Contents

List of Contributors

Dr Mark Batty is a Lecturer in Theatre Studies at the Workshop Theatre, University of Leeds. His interests include the translation and production of contemporary French and Swedish drama. He maintains a healthy curiosity for all things IT and is rarely far from a PC.

Alan Beck is a Lecturer in Drama at the University of Kent. His research interests are radio theory, radio drama, and representations of HIV/AIDS in plays and films. He co-organises the yearly Radio Drama Conference (in Goldsmiths College, London). He has recently published the book *Radio Acting*.

Dr Christie Carson is a Research Fellow in the Department of Drama and Theatre at Royal Holloway University of London. She is co-editor of *The Cambridge King Lear CD-ROM: Text and Performance Archive* and co-founder of the Centre of Multimedia Performance History. She will shortly be commencing as principal investigator on a new ARHB research project entitled *Designing Shakespeare: an audio-visual archive 1960–2000*.

Steve Dixon is Head of Performance at the University of Salford, and Co-Director of the Digital Performance Archive. His IT work includes the production of two CD-ROMs documenting and analysing the work of his multimedia theatre company, *The Chameleons Group*. Both CDs are free, and can be obtained by e-mailing Steve at: S.Dixon@salford.ac.uk

David Hughes is a Senior Lecturer in Contemporary Arts in the Department of Visual and Performing Arts at The Nottingham Trent University and Editor of *liveartmagazine* that has both a print and online presence. His major research interests are digital culture, hybrid and interdisciplinary art practices, collaborative educational environments and collaborative arts practices.

Dr Sophia Lycouris is AHRB Research Fellow in Creative and Performing Arts at The Nottingham Trent University. With a formal background in dance, she researches cross-disciplinary performance and multimedia work (including digital media) with special interest in concepts of body and movement, video as choreography and the use of new technologies (digital and telematics) in choreography. She is artistic director of *kunstwerk-blend interdisciplinary company*. E-mail: sophie.lycouris@ntu.ac.uk

Barry Russell has a British Academy Institutional Research Fellowship at Oxford Brookes University where he works full-time on the application of hypertext and database techniques to theatre-historical scholarship. He is also IT Officer of the Society for French Studies and editor of the WWW Virtual Library for Theatre. Descriptions of, and links to, all his current projects are available at http://barryrussell.net.

Barry Smith is Professor of Digital Arts and Director of The Performing Arts Digital Research Unit at The Nottingham Trent University, and Co-Director of the Digital Performance Archive. His IT work includes the development of the online Live Art Archive and chairing the IT Group of the National Standing Conference of University Drama Departments. E-mail: barry.smith@ntu.ac.uk

Acknowledgements

We would like to thank the following people for their contributions to this guide.

Mark Batty, University of Leeds

Alan Beck, University of Kent

Christie Carson, Royal Holloway University of London

Donald Cooper, Photostage

Steve Dixon, University of Salford

David Hughes, The Nottingham Trent University

Kate Iles, Performing Arts Data Service

Val Kinsler, 100% Proof

Sophia Lycouris, The Nottingham Trent University

Barry Russell, Oxford Brookes University

Damian Robinson, Archaeology Data Service

Barry Smith, The Nottingham Trent University

Section 1: Introduction – Dramatic Forays into IT: working computers with a broom handle
by Barry Smith

1. IT AND LIVE PERFORMANCE

This Guide is noticeably different from its predecessors in the series: for a start it is largely anecdotal. Not so much a manual of '*how* to do it' it is primarily intended to encourage you to use 'it' in the first place, whatever 'it' may be. I have admired the Arts and Humanities Data Service's *Guide to Good Practice* Series since the first ones in Archaeology and History appeared. As I relate briefly in Section 2.3, my first conscious dealings with IT as a new phenomenon within the academic community came via a colleague involved in early archaeology, history and humanities experiments with digital facilities in the early 1980s. Years later the *Guides* which emanated from those scholars, by then well versed in the particular practice of IT applications to their subject domains, were brief, sharp, focused and offered no-nonsense guidance for individuals and organisations involved in the creation, use and maintenance of relevant digital services, resources and applications. Very much to the point and 'fit for purpose' they were eminently usable and direct. But they didn't seem to have a lot to do with 'drama'.

I was therefore slightly bemused, but delighted, when asked to edit a guide aimed at introducing and encouraging development of IT and digital resources amongst my colleagues in the performing arts. 'Performing arts' of course covers a vast range of interests and skills, involving as it does designers, directors, actors and performers, musicians, critics, technicians, analysts, administrators, theorists… And certainly some of these colleagues had made noticeable inroads into highly specialised computer applications, particularly in areas such as musical composition, computer-aided design, stage management and all the spreadsheet and mailing list applications of administration. Archaeologists and historians may have been early starters in the application of IT to their particular fields of study, perhaps only preceded by scientists who understood at least some of its strange workings, and in particular chemists who at one stage seemed to monopolise large tracts of it. But if these were the speed merchants of IT applications in academia then some groups within the performing arts were certainly the recalcitrant late developers. This *Guide* is primarily for them.

That IT seemed to offer little enticement to some individuals working in the performing arts was – and is – not altogether surprising. Performing arts as in theatre/drama/live-art performance, more than any other field of study save perhaps sports, inevitably puts at its core '*live performance*'. Even as we enter the twenty-first century with all the extraordinary IT developments of recent years, 'live performance' is one of the few applications that IT has hardly touched upon. It is of course true that the recent advent of the digitised image – and in particular moving image – sound and vision, webcasting, CD-ROM and DVD – have begun to make inroads across that final frontier. This is especially so – or so the press and sci-fi industry would have us believe – at the more extreme boundaries of current robotics and Artificial Intelligence research. And as these developments have occurred, so the drama/theatre/ performance community has started to take greater notice. This can be verified by briefly noting productions of large-scale theatrical events such as the Robert Wilson/Philip Glass *production, Monsters of Grace* (1998), Laurie Anderson's *Moby Dick* or, at the other end of the scale, the increasing frequency of city festivals in the UK advertised as having both digital and *performative* aspirations, such as Manchester's *Digital Summers*, Sheffield's *Lovebytes* and Nottingham's *Radiator*. But for many these digital/performative experiments are still largely seen as being little different to what video, film and back projection have offered for decades, most frequently an accompaniment to the live act, at worst a distraction or unnecessary special effect. Suspicion about the relationship between the 'live' event and the film/video/ screen event persists, as the old wounds reopened in Philip Auslander's *Liveness* (1999) testifies. All branches of theatre, drama and live performance value highly the simple stunning theatrical moment – even durational performance which in some ways is a quest for it – and that moment, when achieved, is measured in effectiveness rather than complexity. It is equally true that digitally controlled lighting, sound and theatrical effects have become more sophisticated. As a result, the much loved broom-handle technique of simultaneously putting on or off a battery of stage-lights (hitherto a common device in amateur and studio theatres when the lighting rheostats were hot, bulky and unwieldy), or of using a large sheet of metal as a thunder generator may fast be becoming memorabilia and curiosities. But the metal sheet *always* produced the sound of thunder (and some would maintain 'better' thunder!) whereas the small sound-cue button may not always prove quite so reliable or convincing!

If those suspicions exist amongst its core community a good guide must confront them or it's going to be a poor guide. And a central tenet of this *Guide* is to encourage colleagues to consider some of the advantages that digital resources may now proffer and the price which must be paid. The performing arts has not been the only discipline to withhold judgement on whether new is necessarily better: until quite recently significant proportions of the visual arts remained extremely sceptical and in many quarters still is. Hardly surprising, a mere twenty years ago the much heralded technological revolution was incapable of producing a picture worthy of the name. Eager beavers may bring about the future but wiser beavers perhaps wait for it to arrive. Two episodes from those times are burned into my memory. One was my Dean of the School of Art & Design trading his first IT allowance for some extra space – 'We are artists, designers, performers! We have no use for number crunching machines! What we desperately need is more *space*'. He was a textiles expert but clearly should have been an actor. There was a deafening silence until the Dean of Engineering duly obliged by trading an old dishevelled terrapin hut for the extra IT allowance. (That story has now come full circle with the current Dean of Art & Design trading large tracts of design studio space for high-spec Macs for Graphic Design.) The second tale involved a fruitless search for images on the Internet which took me on a pointless trip to York (where a Scottish University Home Page eventually appeared on a flickering screen bearing a black and white crest), and a frustrating afternoon with a computer buff who claimed to have seen images on the Net. This could be described as a near equivalent of the visionary blind-seer and resulted only in the transmission of a cartoon image of a dismal-looking cod from the University of Reykjavik. Trying to console me my colleague opined 'Yes it is a bit disappointing, it doesn't work very well yet... But I think it's going to get better!' She was right.

It has got 'better' and more relevant on all fronts – in its functionality and practicality within performance practice and events, as a medium for studying, recording, analysing and then recording and disseminating conclusions, as a storehouse of research documentation for future generations and, not of least importance to academics and teachers, as a novel and potentially vibrant and massive teaching and learning facility. It is still in its infancy but the signs and future are now increasingly clear: version 1.0 at least has been completed, version 2.0 is well advanced. For performance that much was evident a few years ago when the MIT Professor Janet Murray published *Hamlet on the Holodeck* (1997), investigating the then current and future potential of computer-based performance narrative. Interestingly enough the earliest forms of attempted 'internet theatre' – for example the Oudeis Project, which commenced as early as 1995 (see http://www.oudeis.org/), often and appropriately took classical 'wanderings' as the essential narrative and that is still evident even in current digital performance experiments. The Catalanian solo performance-artist Marcel.li Antunez Roca's most recent performance event Afasia (ICA, London: June 2000) is one such example. Both pieces are based on Homer's *The Odyssey*. The same tendency is still evident in the current webcast experiments in the latest application of technology to performance/media, called 'inhabited television' (where 'audience' can begin to interact with the performers, presented simultaneously both to conventional passive viewers and to online participants). The Mixed Reality Laboratory of The University of Nottingham (see http://www.illumin.co.uk/avatarfarm) recently presented a classical narrative tale of humans versus the gods, played out against a background closely resembling Stonehenge. At this stage both gods and humans are portrayed by avatars and the human variety, interestingly enough, featuring the control and voices of Equity actors.

Mention of Equity actors is not entirely accidental: computer-generated film animations of the *Toy Story* variety (which still fall into the 'drawn cartoon' variety) have more recently given way to common-place assumptions that special effects such as in *Titanic* (1997) and *Star Wars: Episode 1* (1999) have now developed to the point of apparently recreating dead actors (Oliver Reed's final scenes in *Gladiator* (2000), or wholly creating advertising digital divas such as Motorola's 'Mya' complete with fan club. In the light of the recent American actors' strike, advertising executives are beginning to mutter that it might be cheaper to use virtual actors. Perhaps fortunately, that economy is not yet the case but it's an indicator of the pace and direction of development. Those distant tribes and native groups who were teased for not allowing explorers to take their photographs because they believed it would in some way capture their soul might eventually be proved right! Replicants and the predictions of *Blade Runner* (1982) seem ever nearer in the world of theatre, drama and performance.

2. USING IT

As all such developments have occurred with ever increasing rapidity, Higher Education authorities have struggled magnificently to stay abreast and provide their communities with help, guidance and encouragement. These are major shifts and not easily managed as they happen on a national and global scale, involving as they do a mix of new technologies, invention and bewildering applications, not to mention changes of attitude and opportunity. The Arts and Humanities Data Service has been in the thick of it from the outset and two subgroups of particular significance to the performing arts academic community – the Performing Arts Data Service [PADS] and the Visuals Arts Data Service [VADS] – have been established to offer first-hand advice on any digital resource project from its outset. I cannot overstress the importance of contacting them early in the development of an idea which relates to digital resources. Within the performing arts academic community, PADS is the obvious first port of call and, as images and particularly moving images begin to play an ever increasing role in that sector, VADS becomes another source of specialist information and advice. They both have web pages which offer further information on making initial enquiries:

PADS: http://www.pads.ahds.ac.uk/padsNewsCollection
VADS: http://vads.ahds.ac.uk/aboutvads/vads_intro.html

For any individuals unfairly labelled 'computer phobic' I can only offer one insight: it's a myth. Few, if any, are going to avoid an approach, device, technique or resource if they are persuaded that it is genuinely beneficial to them and repays the required investment in time or money or energy. 'Computer phobics' are the wiser beavers not yet persuaded that benefits accrue for the investment required. No-one wants – or 'wanted', it has acquired a certain status as of late – to be labelled a computer phobic. Some computer experts at my own institution tried to be helpful to those they considered ill-informed and ran a course called 'I'm a computer phobic too' and were surprised that it recruited poorly. But faced with such a bewildering barrage of terminology, devices, applications and claims, I suspect everyone is computer phobic at some stage. Certainly the difference between 'computer literacy' and 'computer illiteracy' is one of gradation rather than absolutes; one is reminded of the 1960s sketch 'I am Middle Class: I look up to him. But I look down on him'. For anyone who has felt any inadequacy faced with meaningless technical gobbledygook, I offer them this guidance: the glaze. The glaze is simply a technique of skipping those bits that don't make sense and skimming the words until they seem to fit together again into vaguely meaningful sentences. The equivalent in conversation is an impassive face (try to keep your eyes open!) until the speaker runs out of jargon. This isn't quite as negative as it may sound – the same words recur and by dint of repetition the most frequently recurring ones begin to make sense. You can hasten the process if you so wish by deliberately placing yourself in environments where such terminology is likely to occur – reading this guide for example, or glancing through the IT articles in newspapers, or even listening in on conversations. Just as most people's practical abilities with IT begin with some form of typing or word-processing, moving on to e-mail, moving on to Lists, possibly moving to other applications, as with any language or skill curve it's a relatively easy and painless process providing it's staged. If something occurs that seems too big a step just glaze!

There may be moments in this volume when you will need to glaze but I hope you will find them few and far between. All contributors, including myself, have tried to reduce the technological jargon to acceptable chunks which will be informative to those looking for further detail without causing others to sustain eye damage through over-lengthy glazing. Our combined intention is not conversion but encouragement and I suspect all contributors feel (and some say directly) 'If I did it, you can do it'.

This *Guide* is in fact not the first to acknowledge the increasing interest in the use of digital resources within the performing arts community: that accolade belongs to Mark Batty who authored for the SCUDD IT Group (Standing Conference of University Drama Departments) *A Very Basic Introduction to IT*. Generally known under its diminutive title of 'Idiot's Guide' or more politely 'SCUDD IT Guide' it was distributed free to members of the SCUDD [Association] in 1998/9. The opening sentence of the Foreword marks the same spot: 'Information Technology has become an essential part of all our lives, whether we like it or not. This booklet is for those of us who do not like it...' but by a gentle process of straightforward explanation of the fundamentals – naming of parts, distinguishing between Mac and PC, networking etc. – notes on software, file management and the Internet and an extensive Glossary, it achieved its aim of being an informative booklet 'for the least computer literate without teaching everyone else how to suck their eggs' (Batty, n.d. [1999]). I'm delighted that the excellent Glossary in that booklet has been expanded by Mark Batty for inclusion in this *Guide* and is highly recommended as a plain English explanation of any terminology that is unfamiliar.

A 'Guide' is not a 'Manual' and even though many of the chapters give tips, hints and occasional 'don'ts' – their function is not a step-by-step account of how to *control* IT technology but a step-by-step account of how particular outcomes can be achieved *using* IT technology. And in all cases the framework used for those accounts is one very familiar to dramatists (but never let it be said that I suggested it was the *only* one), that of telling a story. And thus the emphasis on the anecdotal. So each chapter has a standard plot and the plot in each case is of the 'What Katy Did and How She Did It' variety. And whom she met along the way. A common theme of the majority of the contributors is that along the way Katy met a competent technician who could facilitate her chosen production aims, helping to translate her aspirations, designs and intentions into a performance that worked. A common aspect of all contributors, indeed a qualifying necessity, is that they have directed successful projects involving various aspects of digital resources related to the performing arts. In some instances it was for documentation purposes, in some for teaching purposes, in some for research purposes, in some for all three. The strong underlying assumption – that collaboration must play a significant part (with the audience/user, with fellows and colleagues, with technical staff, professionals and specialists) is not an unfamiliar one to the performing arts community which has always recognised that it must use what's possible to make what's extraordinary.

3. IT AND THE PERFORMING ARTS

As editor I have sought to put little restraint on my contributors or even offered them much above the minimum by way of guidance: uniformity of approach was not my intention. Perhaps I have an old-fashioned view of subtle characterisation but I wanted to hear careful scholarship at work as well as an editor in the e-newsroom, the vigorous director at full stretch ('Which one of us is that?' I hear the contributors ask) as well as the more ruminative researcher. Whilst not claiming to be the Prologue to the Canterbury Tales I hope readers will welcome the range of characters, I'm sure you'll find every chapter refreshingly different. Such differences help to undermine the argument that IT requires conformity and mass production – for performing arts creativity that would be pointless, the direction of the performing arts is to create and question rather than obligingly conform. Thus this *Guide* purports to be a reference book you can read straight through!

Editors have the advantage of being able to read all the contributions and draw points from them for the Introduction, thus appearing terribly erudite and learned. Somewhat stupidly this inevitability had never struck me before. But I rather like it. Perhaps the most common characteristic all contributors share as well as their interest in digital resources in performance is a quiet humour – well sometimes not so quiet – that is clearly a valuable resource when things don't quite go according to plan. And with digital resources in their present stage of development, that is probably the biggest certainty of all. I haven't undertaken any psychometric testing of the contributors but it might have been interesting to ascertain their attitude to tragicomedy. If this volume is not exactly a 'warts an' all' revelation, it certainly is not afraid of outlining the disasters as well as the successes, the disadvantages – sometimes with disarming honesty – as well as the satisfying outcomes. It may sometimes appear that digital resources in the performing arts is a bed of roses, as long as you remember that roses tend to have more thorns than blooms. Perhaps surprisingly, finance and budgets do not appear as *the* over-riding feature, although both capital expenditure and revenue costs certainly feature as part of the necessary planning and calculation as an idea is developed. Similarly, those areas where additional expenditure comes as a surprise rather than a calculation are faithfully reported. But in all cases it is the *idea* which is the starting point and not the rather unattractive creamy-grey boxes and tangle of wires which seem to cost a fortune. The over-riding view seems to be that if the idea is useful and workable, then the necessary backing can be secured. And if supply tends to follow 'need' rather than 'demand', there's a strong argument for demonstrating the need.

As digital images have become more easily facilitated and ever more greatly in demand, one key common concern has developed: copyright. An easy way of earning money would be to bet that whenever two or more persons involved with digital resources meet their conversation turns towards copyright within the first two minutes. The subject is not made any easier by the current 'harmonisation' of copyright law currently under discussion within the European Union. Quite how discordant 'harmony' can get before it's no longer harmony I'm unsure but the issue of copyright is likely to test those limits as much as it tests the patience, goodwill and common-sense of anyone who becomes involved with it. Frankly, at the current time and with all the current developments in IT, politics and finance the subject is a mess. As such it is far too complex to detail here, though Christie Carson's brief summary is admirable and her warning to investigate the complications of this particular can of worms earlier rather than later in any project is certainly to be highly recommended. The only useful guidance I can offer readers in need of additional early guidance on the complexities of copyright is first to consult one of the free sources of advice which is recent enough to be current and sufficiently close to the particular problems faced by the arts in the UK to offer appropriate advice.

For a general summary:

Creating Digital Resources for the Visual Arts: Standards and Good Practice
http://vads.ahds.ac.uk/guides/creating_guide/sect23.html

Running throughout all the chapters – sometimes asked directly, sometimes more obliquely – are the same questions: what is the objective? what are the priorities? who are the eventual users? are the eventual users a wider constituency than the initial users and if so is that provision built in? The need and value of pre-planning is stressed by some and the lack of it regretted by others which amounts to the same thing: plan as meticulously as possible and reach firm rather than fudged decisions at each stage. This is after all primarily a binary medium. It understands yes, it understands no, it doesn't so easily understand maybe.

Barry Russell's impressive individual project – if you don't do anything else *do* visit his web site, it's inconceivable that it doesn't hold something of relevance to your interest in performing arts whatever it is – is described in an enviably pithy style full of memorable epigrams and wise tips. He demonstrates just how easy it can be to create a digital resource – so easy that by his account it can be made to look after itself! That's about as wise as it's possible to get! Christie Carson describes her central role in developing a truly massive digital resource and concentrating on both the highs and lows of project management with the intention of increasing the former and decreasing the latter for the next wave of CD-ROM based investigations. Her explorations in what she calls 'a dynamic medium' promises to mark new opportunities for scholarship as well as, in this particular instance, unparalleled investigation of the development of scholarship around one particular play, *King Lear*.

From probably the world's most famous play to some of the world's least known events as recorded in the digital Live Art Archive, the next chapter seeks to demonstrate how digital resources can easily facilitate the widest possible access though the medium of the Internet. The Internet is also a key feature of Alan Beck's account of starting the e-journal *Sound Journal* and achieves the double-whammy of promoting a relatively under-used facility on a definitely under-credited dramatic medium, radio.

David Hughes' contribution takes us into another little-used and little understood aspect of digital resources: the Intranet. And, brave man that he is, he uses it directly as a teaching facility for undergraduates and faithfully recounts the ups and downs of this on-going development. Though this particular digital approach may be new to many, his struggle with gremlins and increased student numbers, inadequate equipment and frustrating delays will be all too familiar. Readers of a romantic disposition may even hear distant thunder emanating from those daily press reports of the development of e-universities by commercial entrepreneurs or note with interest the vast explosion of world educational multimedia conferences (a current one, 'World Conference on Educational Multimedia, Hypermedia & Educational Telecommunications' is advertising 'Over 600 Presentations in 33 Topic Strands'. Hypermedia indeed!) But David demonstrates that the quality of engagement and motivation can still be pre-eminent and that digital resources can support pedagogic aims rather than be technology driven.

The third and final section parallels two 'similar but different' developments, one in theatre, one in dance. Steve Dixon's *Chameleons 2* CD-ROM has already achieved something of a model status as a digital resource being an *outcome* of a theatre production (which itself involved extensive use of multimedia). The concentric ordering of layers of information and observation from the play to broad contemporary theories comfortably spans documentation, developing a teaching resource and undertaking detailed research. Three digitally dependent experiments which have recently occurred in dance productions form the core of Sophia Lycouris' contribution and from which she extracts the two most central, if most difficult questions: what is the *relationship* of live presence to digital technology? How does the technology *mediate* the live experience? These are key inter-related issues with significant implications for the future development of theatre/drama/performance both as a practice or event and as an academic subject.

As I put the finishing touches to this volume I have come to realise that there is at least one chapter missing – well several in fact, but I am presupposing that designers, musicians and theatre technicians will be developing their own specialist 'good guides' in due course. My missing chapter is an account by a practitioner using old antiquated digital resources that are well past their sell-by date but which are given new purpose with a modicum of lateral thinking and a lot of imagination. That moment of metamorphosis, transition and improvisation is endemic to the performing arts and would have proved most popular; I apologise for its omission. By the time such developments are commonplace and accounts conventionally published we might all be undertaking as a matter of routine various versions of the humanoid experiments of performance artists like Stelarc, when he physically wires himself into the Internet. But by then death, at least according to current sci-fi, will have been banished: digital resources evidently still have some way to go!

Section 2: Digital Resources in Performance Studies

2.1: Running a web site – How to design, build and maintain a database-powered web site
by Barry Russell

1. DOING IT OURSELVES

The first time I searched the web for 'Racine' all I got was a list of pumpkin-growers in Racine County, Wisconsin. It's easy to be disappointed.

We may miss what we're looking for entirely, even though it's out there. We may retrieve a fair number of relevant items, but find them buried in a mass of irrelevant material. How can we improve the situation?

The short answer is that we could search among resources that have already been filtered by someone who knows the subject area – we could use a subject-specific gateway, a portal. The more precisely focused the portal, the better will be the returns we get from it. PADS, the Performing Arts Data Service, is building such a portal (http://www.pads.ahds.ac.uk/padsTheatreCollection).

When the British physicist Tim Berners-Lee, inventor of the web, first thought about this problem a decade ago, he came up with the idea of the WWW Virtual Library (http://www.vlib.org). The plan was to create a master-catalogue of good resources, organised on a loose hierarchical tree structure, where each part of the tree was maintained by a volunteer. If you were interested in the theatre, for example, you'd start at the humanities, go to arts, then performing arts, then theatre. In an ideal world, he'd have come up with a systematic classification system, something like the Dewey Decimal System or the Library of Congress system. But back in those early days, nobody really expected the growth that actually happened, and the first volunteer maintainers were largely left to their own devices.

What we have now is an Internet whose growth is being driven by a wide variety of factors, and an increasingly overwhelming amount of material which it is difficult to navigate through without the use of specialised gateways. The kind of material and organisation we are going to need in the future is beginning to emerge, but in a piecemeal, fragmented fashion.

We can intervene as individuals to try to change this. By diverting some of the energies we have traditionally spent creating scholarly resources on *paper* into creating resources *online*, we could help to shape the working environment of the next generation. If the portal we want doesn't exist, we can create it.

This section offers some guidelines on how you might get started. The key point is to think of the task of creating web sites, not in terms of web technology alone, but as a combination between the web and a second technology: the database.

1.1. A powerful combination

When you link a database engine to a web server you get a powerful combination that can deliver many kinds of scholarly project.

This is the combination behind the World Wide Web Virtual Library for Theatre (http://vl-theatre.com), which now attracts over a million hits a year and grows under its own impetus with very little maintenance. Similar techniques drive the European Internet Resource Guide at Oxford Brookes University (http://solinux.brookes.ac.uk/rg/top.php3). They also provide the chronologies of French theatre and the bibliography of theatre scholarship that underpin the hypertext study of Parisian fairground theatre (http://foires.net). They lie at the heart of a major new international project called CESAR, a comprehensive survey of plays, performers, theatre spaces and publications in France during the 17th and 18th centuries that will be available online soon.

1.2. Getting started

A good resource guide takes time to develop. In the early stages it's best kept away from the light, like a small plant. You will know when it's ready to make public. The time you spend getting it right in the privacy of your own workspace will repay you many times later. Nobody will know how long you laboured. When you go public, if you've been successful, your project will look as clean and fresh as if it had sprung full-grown from Jupiter's side that same day.

It helps, when you begin, to have a concentric model in your mind of what it is you hope to achieve. Build from the centre out, so that you preserve an appearance of unity and integrity at all points. My first chronology of French theatre listed only popular fairground plays during a 15-year span between 1700 and 1715. Later it became 'Theatre in the Age of Louis XIV' (1660–1715) (Fig. 1). In its next incarnation, it will cover all performance arts in France between 1600 and 1800 – and it will no longer be mine, but the combined work of nearly a dozen scholars around the world. Perhaps it will grow even further, for it will no longer be limited to what I can do myself: it will have a life of its own.

The kernel of your project should be something you care about. Indifference makes for dull work, and enthusiasm enlivens it. Begin with a topic you know well, where your personal slant will give your work a distinctive sparkle. As the project grows, your claim to be an authority in the area will come under ever closer scrutiny. The stronger your claim, the more easily you will attract collaboration. At some stage the survival of your site may depend on the extent to which colleagues recognise it as authoritative.

One insight that came to me early in my experiments with hypertext is that it's easier to change the label than to change the content. There is no point in calling something a guide to world theatre if 95% of the resources refer to North America. Call it what it is, and change the label later. Never be ashamed of what you can't include, for you're probably the only one who

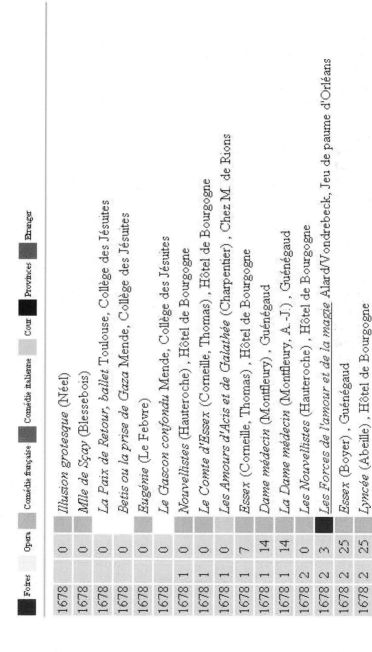

Calendrier électronique des spectacles sous l'Ancien Régime

Année 1678

	Foires	Opera	Comédie française	Comédie italienne	Cour	Provinces	Etranger		
1678	0								Illusion grotesque (Néel)
1678	0								Mlle de Sçay (Blessebois)
1678	0								La Paix de Retour, ballet Toulouse, Collège des Jésuites
1678	0								Betis ou la prise de Gaza Mende, Collège des Jésuites
1678	0								Eugénie (Le Febvre)
1678	0								Le Gascon confondu Mende, Collège des Jésuites
1678	1								Nouvellistes (Hauteroche) , Hôtel de Bourgogne
1678	1								Le Comte d'Essex (Corneille, Thomas) , Hôtel de Bourgogne
1678	1								Les Amours d'Acis et de Galathée (Charpentier) , Chez M. de Rions
1678	1								Essex (Corneille, Thomas) , Hôtel de Bourgogne
1678	1								Dame médecin (Montfleury) , Guénégaud
1678	1								La Dame médecin (Montfleury, A.-J.) , Guénégaud
1678	2								Les Nouvellistes (Hauteroche) , Hôtel de Bourgogne
1678	2								Les Forces de l'amour et de la magie Alard/Vondrebeck, Jeu de paume d'Orléans
1678	2								Essex (Boyer) , Guénégaud
1678	2								Lyncée (Abeille) , Hôtel de Bourgogne
1678	2								Le Comte d'Essex (Boyer) , Guénégaud
1678	3								Circé en postures Alard/Vondrebeck, Jeu de paume d'Orléans

Figure 1: An illustration of the Chronology of French Theatre

knows what's missing (and what's coming), if you've been wise with your labels. Work on the web almost always looks complete, even though it's never finished. That's one of the characteristics that distinguishes it from paper-based work: you can't see the boundaries.

When I first began to build the Virtual Library for Theatre, I spent many weeks searching the Internet, trawling for resources, assessing what was out there, before I dared to settle on a first set of categories, flesh them out, and go public. Other projects need different sorts of preparation. Creating my chronologies involved digging through many volumes of printed sources before anything at all could appear online. Only when that had been done could I add the feature that made it a native web project: hyperlinks to online versions of the plays listed (http://foires.net/cal/cal1678.shtml).

2. PLANNING FOR GROWTH

One prime consideration is that the model should be capable of further growth. This is something you don't have with paper – unless, like Dostoievsky or Dickens, you start a serialised novel without knowing how it will end. On the Internet, there's no need for an end, especially when it's a resource guide you're building, where the sites you refer to come and go with a sometimes discouraging velocity. You can plan for indefinite growth. This means, for example, that one could start by listing all the online theatre companies in the world in a single alphabetical sequence by company name. When the list reaches a certain mass, it becomes inevitable that it should sub-divide into groups by country. Soon, maybe, I'll have to re-sort my lists by continent. When we colonise the Moon, I'll have to think again.

2.1. Collaboration

Another factor you can't always foresee when you begin a project is the possibility that you yourself will sub-divide, as it were. You may take on collaborators – as assistants, if you're that way inclined, or as partners, if you like to share and believe in the benefits to be gained from encounters between equals. It doesn't always work. I whole-heartedly believed, when I started the Virtual Library for Theatre, that it would quickly become a team effort. Four years and several million hits down the road, it's still just me. Thankfully, building in a good feedback loop with the users, and using some simple automated maintenance techniques, has meant I've still had time to earn a living with my day job.

Collaboration, though, is something you should plan for, if your project has any serious growth potential. We often begin our first databases or web projects with just ourselves in mind. We cut corners, 'cheat', don't bother to impose consistency on ourselves, because we don't think anybody else is ever going to see the inner workings, and so it won't matter. But, given the current trends in online scholarship, and the huge potential for convergence in the future, not to mention the sheer joy of online collaborative endeavours, it's worth being tough with yourself now so that you get – and give – an easy ride further down the road.

If you build a database, think good and hard about the fields you need. Some day you may regret that you lumped first and last names together, or didn't stick to a consistent pattern in entering dates. If in doubt, break it down. It is much easier to combine two fields when you build your web page than to divide a field that contains more than you need.

If it's a web site you want, take the time to learn at least the rudiments of writing good, clean code, so that you, or your future collaborators, can take your code and reshape it to fit new contexts or answer new needs. Use the AHDS guides (http://ahds.ac.uk/public/guides.html) and other resources that are there to help you. I wish I had. There are HTML pages buried in some of my web sites that embarrass and frustrate me now. Updating them to take account of labour-saving style sheets or the new techniques for handling structured information on the web (like XML) is a nightmare. The AHDS handout, 'Creating a Viable Scholarly Data Resource' (http://ahds.ac.uk/deposit/viable.html), would have saved me months of work if it had been available when I, and some of my collaborators, first started. Work as if in public, even when you work in private.

2.2. Working with users

Think of your users as collaborators, too. Many of the best resources listed in the Virtual Library for Theatre have come not from me, but from people visiting the site. In part this is designed. I never build a web site now without providing for user recommendations. It is one of the keys to sustainable development. In principle, some of my sites could now run – and grow – with zero input from me. They might evolve forever, if only I could find a way to drop out of the chain and channel the small income my site makes in book sales royalties from Amazon.com directly to my Internet Service Provider. In practice it isn't quite that simple, since even the best-intentioned can make mistakes filling in the online form and submit a broken link; while the worst-intentioned could drive a whole sex industry through the security loophole of an unattended submission form. The system I have is a compromise. Every online submission triggers an e-mail alert that I see within seconds (if I'm connected), so I can correct errors, kill anything offensive, and occasionally write to thank someone for their contribution.

How much you interact with your site's users off-screen is a matter of personal choice. Theatre is one of those fields where enthusiasm and interest are usually high. The user spectrum runs the range from stage-struck adolescents who want the quickest way to Broadway to retired academics anxious to stay in touch with that little corner of the field that is forever theirs. If you have a taste for e-mail, and enjoy building virtual friendships, you can get tremendous pleasure and give real service by responding to whatever queries come in. I answer 20 or 30 a week. It gives me a feel for where the site is going, and helps to build a quality of what tradespeople call 'customer relations' that would be the envy of many corporate pages. If you can't afford the time, or don't have the inclination, do what the professionals do: at least make your automated replies *seem* personal. Interaction on the web is always best when it's closest to one-to-one. (Fig. 2)

3. SOFTWARE

The database came late in my development of the Virtual Library for Theatre. For a longer time than I care to remember, every link was painfully added by hand with the usual searching inside a dense text for the right place to put the angle brackets and the usual fumbling with the shift key and double quotes. It was hard work, and it took too long. I had to change when people started to complain that the link they'd suggested in March still wasn't there in September. Sometimes the e-mails got quite tart.

Recommendation form

30 Mar 2000

Here's where you can recommend pages you think are worth including.

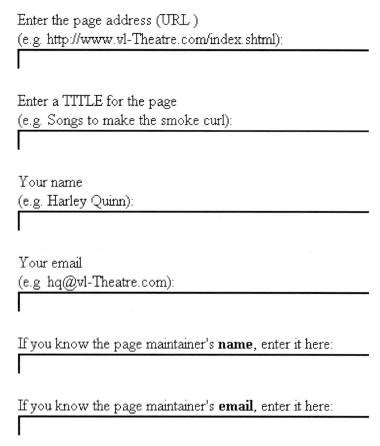

Figure 2: Example of an online feedback form

The tools you need to build projects like the Virtual Library for Theatre are available at little or no cost. They span different operating systems. Once set up, they run with little maintenance. The techniques for handling them are normally well documented. A handful of simple programming routines is enough to get you started. You may need technical help to put your system in place and do the initial configuration, but it is surprising how far you can get with a good book and an online help file. We are blessed, as the first generation to have the opportunity to use these tools. But we have to invest a little time and effort in learning how to use them. It's not that different from the problem an earlier generation faced, when academics had to learn how to type.

My first attempt at web/database interaction relied on Microsoft Access and a programming system based on Visual Basic called ASP ('Active Server Pages') (http://msdn.microsoft.com/library/backgrnd/html/msdn_aspfaq.htm). The combination is still popular and it has the great virtue of being available to anyone who has a copy of the Microsoft Office suite and the Personal Web Server that comes with Windows. It's perfect for building projects like bibliographies on your own desktop. It's capable of powering substantial online sites, like the National Residence Abroad Database (http://nrad.fdtl.ac.uk/nrad/qaintro.htm). But if you are committing to going public, if you're thinking ahead to collaboration, if you're expecting your site to grow in size or complexity, and if you want to work to tight budget constraints, it's not the combination I would recommend.

There are three elements to think about: the web server, the database engine, and the programming language. I chose Apache, MySQL and PHP.

Apache is the most popular web server in the world. One reason is that it is free. You can download it from the Internet (http://www.apache.org/httpd.html) and install it easily on Windows or on UNIX. It takes up little space and few resources: you can run it on your desktop, or even on your laptop. The bundled documentation addresses the needs of all users, from the absolute beginner to the most discriminating systems manager.

MySQL is a database management system (DBMS). It is comparable in power to commercial systems such as Oracle and Microsoft SQL Server, but costs nothing to educational users. Again, you can download it from the Internet (http://www.mysql.com) for use on Windows or on UNIX.

PHP is the programming language I use to control the way my web pages interact with my database. Other languages are possible (e.g. Perl), but PHP is immensely powerful, easy to understand and use, and has been tailor-made to perform just this interactive web role. Its full name is 'Personal Hypertext Preprocessor', which means you can use it to build *instructions* into your web page rather than just plain text and formatting. The instructions are processed before the web page is delivered. Download it from the mother site (http://www.php.net) or from your nearest mirror site – the home page will tell you where that is.

4. THE BARE BONES

It takes less than an hour to set up these three applications. Step-by-step instructions are available online (http://www.devshed.com/Server_Side/Administration/Database/). Once you have them running, you can create the bare bones of a database-driven web project by following these steps:

Decide your data structure. What fields will you need?
- Create your database tables.
- Design your web pages. Add forms with fields that correspond to the fields in your database when you want to capture data; add PHP instructions to read data from the database when you want to display it.

- Put your web pages on the web server.
- Point your browser at your web server and go.

Once you can handle these steps, you can move on to designing whole web sites that run from a database. The layout of your pages, the styles used within them, the graphics, links and all other content can be generated on the fly from simple menu-driven options on a single web page. If you add to that the routines needed to collect new data from users, it becomes possible to build a self-sustaining web site with many pages that requires almost no further input from you. The European Resource Guide at Oxford Brookes (http://solinux.brookes.ac.uk/rg/top.php3) runs this way. I haven't touched it since I created it.

5. LOOKING FOR SUCCESS

What makes the difference between a successful project and a poor one? I wish I knew. What I like about my favourite sites is best expressed in aesthetic rather than in technical or strategic terms. I like simplicity, clarity, elegance, harmony. Maybe these qualities register with the users of a site and help to make it popular. Or perhaps the qualities I'm calling aesthetic actually have hard-boiled procedural equivalents that we could talk about without poetics. 'Simple' becomes well planned, 'clear' becomes easy to read, 'elegant' might mean that it's easy to navigate, 'harmonious' could be no more than the desire not to overfill a space or overextend a list when it reaches the point where it could be sub-divided.

Dulce et utile is still sound. It doesn't matter how pleasing a site is to use if nobody uses it. One key to success is spotting an opportunity in the market and doing something to fill it.

We need the top-level portals, that's for sure. But we also need comparable resources all the way down the food chain – specialised groupings of sub-categories, national and regional listings, genre collections – down to the stuff that really counts, the original material that is available nowhere else, and in no other form. When we have that, and we have the portals to help us find it, we can claim the Internet has matured in our sector. It's up to our generation to make that happen.

2.2: Creating a multipurpose research tool for the study of *King Lear*
by Christie Carson

Over the past four years I have worked on the *Cambridge King Lear CD-ROM: Text and Performance Archive*. The purpose of this section is to use this process as a case study to take you through the process of managing a digital project of this size and scale. Initially, the creation of a multimedia project was likened to creating a digital library of material. More realistically, however, it has been compared with the creation of a small feature film. In keeping with this second description I will divide the process into four phases: 1) Planning and design 2) Research 3) Production and 4) Post-production. By tracing the *Lear* project through these four phases it will be possible to outline the overall structure of such a project, allowing me to divide my advice for project management into discrete sections.

1. PLANNING AND DESIGN

There is a maxim in film-making that every dollar spent in pre-production is worth two spent in production. This is very sound advice when it comes to the planning of a multimedia project of any size, regardless of the budget. Careful planning and a clear design, which includes a well-defined intellectual framework, is an essential starting point for any project which is to succeed.

1.1. Creating a framework

Part of the intellectual framework must be a reason (or several) for doing the project in this format in the first place. For the *Lear* project there were three. The first was to create a new edition of the play through the creation of the Finder Text. The second justification for a digital project was to draw together materials about the play that could be reassembled in different ways, thereby drawing together the work of two separate disciplines. The third underlying justification for this project has been to take advantage of another strength of this medium, giving access to information which would otherwise not be available to students or researchers not able to visit London, Stratford-upon-Avon, Washington or New York. In order to collect this material I spent a full year in research libraries, where I was admitted only after obtaining a reader's card which was offered to me because of this specific project. This is not a means by which to encourage discovery. Through this project I hope that students and scholars will encounter materials but also ideas and approaches which they would not normally come across. If your reasons for doing a project in this medium are not absolutely clear and compelling it may be sensible to find another means to express your ideas. A book will always be easier, quicker and more certain.

Turning to the *King Lear* project, I will start by outlining the fundamental premise which underpins the archive. The issue at the centre of this research tool is a desire to highlight the fact that this text has had as many variations as it has had performances. The key aim of the project, therefore, is to highlight the fluidity of the text over time. As a result, it was agreed that the material presented had to illustrate performance variations through printed text, performance history support material and a database of illustrations relating to the play in performance.

In order to illustrate temporal fluidity, a structural model for the project was developed. Therefore, at the centre of the project are two timelines. The first is the timeline of the play. The second is the historical timeline of performance. In order to illustrate both of these progressions of time, it was decided the illustrations of performance would be displayed both chronologically and by act and scene. In order to draw all of the information about the play together it was also decided that the text itself would become a navigational tool. The Finder Text, which has become the backbone of the project, is a conflation of the Quarto and Folio texts. This text, which I have created myself, is an extensively hypertexted new edition of the play which has linked to it all the commentary notes and apparatus from the *New Cambridge Shakespeare* edition of the play and the staging notes from Jacky Bratton's *Plays in Performance* edition. As a conflated text was used for performance for the hundred and fifty years after Macready reinstated the Shakespearean text (from 1834 to the mid 1980s) it was seen as essential to have an edition of the play which could reflect that performance tradition. This new text is unique in that it offers a conflated text which highlights in different colours those lines present only either in the Quarto or the Folio. As a result it provides an unprecedented means of studying the textual variations in the play. Unlike formerly published parallel texts, this new Finder text will combine all of the information into a single text which is supported by further links to information from Jay Halio's textual analysis (Fig. 3).

1.2. Deciding on the design

Assuming that you do wish to proceed and you now know what you are doing and why, it is possible to move on to how it must be done. When creating projects of this kind, particularly in the context in which I am working (that is with one of the most revered canonical texts to be published by one of the most respected academic presses) it is essential to look at the suppositions which underlie the work you are doing. In some respects I have replicated old forms of scholarship in a new medium. I have created a new, slightly more convenient, edition of the play. But I hope I have done more. Through providing additional material which supports or possibly gives the user evidence to question that traditional scholarship, I hope that I have exposed traditional scholarship to scrutiny. Also, by bringing together the approaches of textual and performance scholars, I hope to have opened the door to a new hybrid form of research in this area which draws on the strengths of both of these established forms.

The hypertext links which I have used in the *King Lear* CD-ROM project are designed to replicate existing methods of connecting information but also to introduce new forms. How this model differs from the model which is used by online dictionaries and encyclopaedias is in the

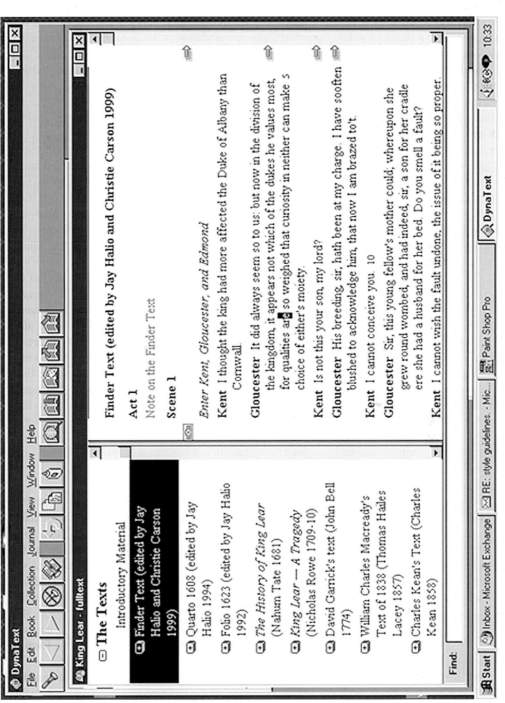

Figure 3: The Finder Text, as edited by Christie Carson and Jay Halio, acts as a navigational device for the CD as a whole. Reproduced with the permission of Cambridge University Press

fact that, while some conclusions are presented, there is room for further research and also sufficient material on the disk to challenge the conclusions of the experts presented. The CD has been laid out in a linear way because this is the only way in which Dynatext will display information, with a Table of Contents down the left margin. But as with any research tool, the user is not expected to read it in a linear fashion. As I have already noted, the play itself has been used as an additional navigational device and the search engine present in the software allows for all manner of additional personalised pathways through the materials.

This project addresses, in an indirect way, two of the points which are at the root of hypertext theory and practice. The first is the idea of creating an active user. In the *Lear* CD there are an almost infinite number of pathways through the material. The users get to decide on the pathways they will take and are spurred on by their interests not by what I, as editor, have chosen to put before them next. The second point which is raised is whether or not the same information *is* the same information if the route to it is different. When designing non-linear projects of this kind it is essential to make information available in a way that makes sense in any order. Is coming upon a passage in Tate's text which differs greatly from the Shakespearean text the same if you find it on your own or if you go there through a guided link? The framework you have created must find concrete form in a design plan.

1.3. Deciding on the content

Once the intellectual framework and design structure are in place it is possible to determine the materials which will be needed to accomplish the intended outcome successfully. In the case of the *Lear* project this resulted in a decision to include ten full texts of the play. Seven of these are encoded digital texts: the *New Cambridge Shakespeare* Edition of the Quarto and the Folio, both edited by Jay Halio, the Tate Adaptation of 1681, the Rowe Edited edition of 1709, Garrick's performance text as recorded in the Bell edition of 1773, Macready's performance text recorded in Lacy's edition of 1857 and Charles Kean's performance text which he published in 1858. Two of these full texts would appear as facsimile images of the original editions; the Trinity College Cambridge copy of the Quarto of 1608 and the Hinman selection of the Folio of 1623 supplied by the Folger Shakespeare Library. The final text to be included was, of course, the extensively hypertexted new edition of the play, the Finder Text.

In addition to the texts and their notes which support the texts, it was decided that the archive would contain an extensive database of performance information. This would include a list of English language performances from 1605 to 1998 and a database of images relating to the play in performance from 1738 to 1998. A series of five essays which detail the textual and performance history of the play would form the critical section of the disk. Finally, additional reference material was added, including biographies of actors, directors and writers, productions reviews and bibliographic information to support further research on the subject.

1.4. Combining structure with content – defining the audience

The audience is something you should think about when you create your framework: however, you will be forced to reassess that audience as you make content and design choices. In the *Lear* example, as a result of the decisions made about the design structure and content, the archive contains only text and still images. Time, money and copyright restrictions made the use of sound and moving images impossible on this project. These were not, of course, the only issues considered when this choice was made. In fact there are a number of strong underlying philosophical reasons for this choice. First, as the aim of the project was to show multiple performance texts, it was seen as essential that no one performance be highlighted or given greater weight through audio or visual representation. Second, as this archive documents the entire history of the play's performance it was felt that those performances which took place before recording equipment was invented should not be so disadvantaged in their representation against more recent productions. By choosing to use text and still images it has been possible to document the entire four hundred year history in a manner which is relatively even-handed. Finally, the vast majority of the moving images available were from television and film adaptations of the play rather than theatrical performances. It was decided from the outset that while film and television adaptations would be documented alongside other representations and adaptations of the play, they would not be highlighted and certainly should not be confused with theatrical performances, the main focus of the archive. Given that our intended audience was university English and Drama Departments the emphasis placed on textual information and still images relating to performance was deemed both appropriate and manageable (Fig. 4).

1.5. Creating a budget

Once you have a clear sense of the framework, design, content and audience you must turn your attention to practical concerns. Two things are essential to recognise from the outset in terms of budgeting such projects; multimedia projects are expensive and time consuming. It is essential to acknowledge that research resources in the performing arts have a market value. Educational projects in this area, while worthy, may not receive the kind of exceptions which other forms of academic publishing have seen. The copyright holders in our area have made a concerted effort over the four years of my work on the CD to create pricing policies which reflect use. Nevertheless, it is important to approach the budgeting of such a project from a realistic position.

Unlike the creation of a book or other scholarly project a budget is essential from the outset. Budgets must realistically assess the value of staff time which will be spent on the project. Often academics do not value their own time sufficiently. However, given that digital projects can take untold hours of work it is important to place parameters on your time and the time of anyone else working on the project. Often the capital expense of equipment is seen as the most important cost in such projects when in fact the main expenditure categories will be salaries, training costs or the cost of buying in expertise and consumable costs, including pursuing cul de sacs of various kinds.

To generalise, the main areas of expenditure which you will have to cover in any project are equipment, research expenses, training, external expertise, purchasing copies of research materials, digitisation expenses, publication permission fees and staff time.

Multimedia projects of any size or scale should be approached professionally. Grants are available from a number of sources to cover costs – the Arts and Humanities Research Board, Lottery Funding and the Leverhume Trust to name a few – but all these sources will expect a realistic budget breakdown and report of expenditure. Do not underestimate the labour-intense nature of such projects or the special skills required. At every stage it will be necessary to balance the cost of paying for outside expertise and services versus buying equipment and

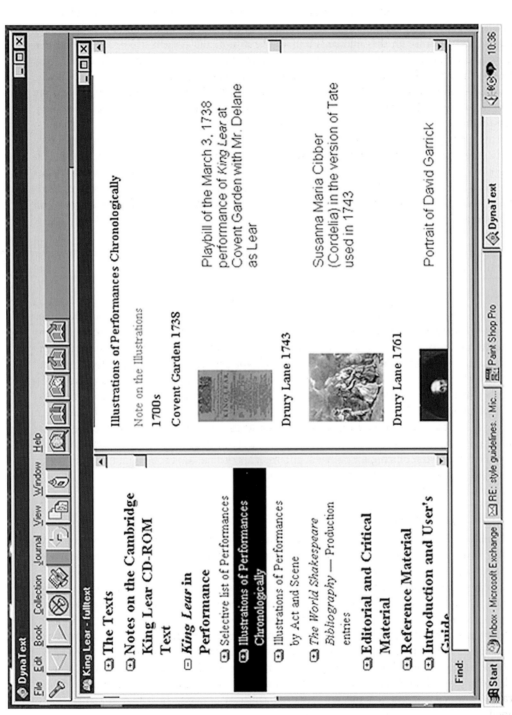

Figure 4: The image database is accessible through the Finder Text, at the beginning of each scene and through the Table of Contents where the images are listed both chronologically, as seen here, and by Act and Scene. Reproduced with the permission of Cambridge University Press

training staff to do the work yourselves. Try to be realistic about your own strengths and weaknesses and budget accordingly.

I cannot stress enough the importance of the first five steps in this process: i) creating a framework, ii) deciding on the design, iii) defining the content, iv) defining the audience, and v) creating a budget. If the structure, design and overall plan for the content are not clear it will be very difficult to proceed with any degree of confidence. If you do not have a sense of your audience and a clearly defined budget a great deal of time and money can be wasted chasing materials that you *might* use. If you think through the project's aims and objectives clearly from the outset you should be in a position to pursue only those materials which you really want. In terms of the film analogy, what you really want at the end of your planning phase is a storyboard, a production schedule and a detailed audience profile. The analogy breaks down, however, when you look at the materials which are wasted in the production process of film. Ideally, with a careful planned multimedia project you should end up with very little on the cutting room floor.

2. RESEARCH

Now that you know what you want to do and how you want to achieve it you can move to the next phase, research. The research process involves two interrelated processes. First, it is essential to locate the materials you want. Second, it is imperative to determine whether these materials can be licensed for reproduction in the form you want them. As problems at this stage arise, and they invariably will, it simplifies matters if you can return to your carefully structured aims and objectives to weigh up decisions about inclusion of material. In many ways copyright is one of the largest hurdles you will have to overcome and for this reason I have dedicated a special section to this. Another issue which is important to address is the notion of balance. As you determine the availability of materials it is important to chart your progress to determine the overall image of the mosaic you are creating. Research requires attention to detail and each item you collect may require special arrangements. This should not distract you, however, from the aim of creating a unified whole in the final project.

2.1. Locating materials

Once the design framework was in place for the *Lear* Archive it was possible to begin in earnest the process of bringing together the materials chosen. The research phase of the project, while long and at times tortuous, was fairly straightforward in its methods. For the image database it was necessary to obtain readers' cards and visit the reading rooms of a range of major Shakespearean and theatre archives. Once *in situ* it was usually essential to make quick and binding decisions. This was a slightly tricky process at the beginning as it was, in essence, starting at the elephant's toe but it became easier as the archive began to take shape. Depending on the scope of the project and the accessibility of the archives involved, it might well be possible to start with a pilot project. This was our initial aim with the CD, starting with Act 1 Scene 1, but it quickly became apparent that it would double the work and the expense to travel to distant archives more than once and, therefore, this initial pilot scheme was dropped in favour of collecting all the materials from the outset.

I was able to create the performance database for the *Lear* project by ordering copies of images from the Theatre Museum, the British Film Institute Library, the Shakespeare Centre Library in Stratford and the private library of the theatre photographer Donald Cooper in this country, and the Folger Shakespeare Library, the New York Public Library, the Harvard Theatre Collection and the Stratford Festival Archives in North America. Ordering the images which I wanted was usually uncomplicated. Determining the ownership of copyright and then applying for permission to publish these images was often much more difficult. Also as I was working with different copyright laws in each of the countries where the performances took place, it often meant a different set of rules for each production and even for individual images. The copyright regulations in this country have changed since the late 1980s so that copyright no longer resides with the commissioning theatre as it did before but with the photographer after first use. You are required to know or to learn the copyright implications of using materials. Ignorance cannot be used as an excuse (Fig. 5).

2.2. Dealing with copyright

Copyright does not only cover the ownership of the image; with creative products there is also the issue of moral rights. Any actor, director, designer, props maker, etc. could object to the use of an image on the grounds that it does not represent their work in a positive light. They would not be entitled to any remuneration for the publication of the image but they could prevent you from using it. In selecting images it is always sensible to choose first those images which have the clearest possible copyright holders; ideally holders who you know are willing to negotiate permission at reasonable prices. If you suspect that copyright might prove difficult, I suggest that it is sensible to have alternative materials in mind if your first choices become unavailable.

Another tip when going through the process of clearing copyright is that you should always think about all of the possible uses for the image that you might have in future and negotiate them all at once rather than having to go back to people time and again. Before permission is granted, you will have to supply very clear details about the number of copies of the project product which will be produced and the intended audience. Again, if your planning phase is carried out carefully you will not have any difficulty in answering these questions.

In general, I would suggest putting copyright clearance at the top of your list of things to get started on when you begin the research phase of the project. You will find that it will take longer than you think to get responses and if you wait until the last minute you may incur unacceptable delays. More importantly, however, you will have to go back to the drawing board if you have designed your project around materials that are not available. Essentially I suggest that you should worry about copyright constantly at the beginning of your project but then think less and less about it as you near completion. If you have done your work, i.e. tried to contact the copyright holder a number of times and can support your actions with letters held on file, then you will be seen to have fulfilled your due diligence legally. It is some comfort to know that copyright infringements only become a problem if the copyright holder decides to sue. In the majority of cases a settlement can be reached without that happening. In the event of someone suing you, a successful copyright suit will award the owner damages to cover lost income, which will probably be negligible in the case of an educational product.

The textual material used in this project came from sources where the copyright was very clear. The additional texts of the play we were able to licence from Chadwyck-Healey who

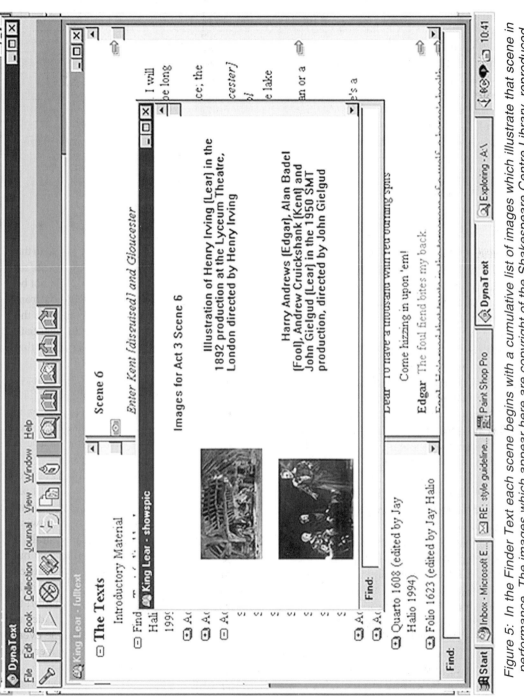

Figure 5: In the Finder Text each scene begins with a cumulative list of images which illustrate that scene in performance. The images which appear here are copyright of the Shakespeare Centre Library, reproduced with the permission of Cambridge University Press

have published the *Shakespeare: Editions and Adaptations* database. Much of the other textual material came from Cambridge University Press. Access to materials which Cambridge held the copyright for was one of the key advantages of working through the Press.

If what you are creating is an in-house project which will only be used by students, you may get away with using educational exceptions. However, if there is any chance that the project could have commercial distribution, even if that distribution is only in the form of payment by students for use, or will be accessible to a wider public, it is essential to sort out the copyright position of *every* item included. Working in the performing arts we are in a difficult position as it should be our job to support and encourage performing artists. Some might say that by putting the work of an artist in your digital project you are supporting him/her. The artist might, however, see that as exploitation if you have not paid him/her for the privilege. It is a fine line that you have to tread.

3. PRODUCTION

Having covered the issues of design and collection of material there leaves only the most frustrating yet most rewarding part of the process, creating the final digital project. If you have designed your project well it will just be a matter of executing your plans. If, like me, you are trying something that you have never done before you may well find that you run into all manner of problems as you go along. At every stage it is important to approach hurdles as opportunities to confirm or abandon your original design ideas. It is important to be flexible about the form your project takes while still hanging on to your original aims, objectives and intellectual framework. If you cannot get there by the method you originally planned there may well be a close approximation which will work. Being clear about your intellectual goals makes this kind of decision easier. Invariably the final project will be the result of some compromise. It is important not to lose heart and to adjust your expectations to what can be achieved, letting go of the perfect vision of the project which was in your head before you knew what was involved.

3.1. Adapting materials

The images for the *Lear* project arrived in three different forms: as prints, slides and digitised images. For each image it was essential to create an archive digital file, which we did using the uncompressed TIFF format. Having this storehouse of source material means that if an image is corrupted in the process of adaptation for the final project it is not necessary to rescan it. For our project it was necessary to create another digital file for each image which was correctly sized for the screen as a GIF image, the file format supported by the Dynatext reader used by Cambridge. File names for the images must be distinct, intelligible and, ideally, no more than eight characters (particularly if you find yourself working with an unhelpful software like Dynatext which will accept nothing else). The same file names were used in the *Lear* project when creating picture captions to enable the two pieces of information to be linked together.

The majority of the textual material arrived in digital form. The texts of the play which were licensed from Chadwyck-Healey, however, used an entirely different set of mark-up codes than we were using ourselves, which caused all manner of problems. The other textual material which came either from Cambridge or directly from the creators of that material also arrived in a variety of formats and used a variety of different conventions. All of this material had to be converted for our purposes on the disk. Conversion of data is a long and meticulous process. It is important when you get material in digital form to think long and hard about whether it will be faster to generate the material from scratch or convert it from other formats. The conventions used in hard-copy publishing are very different from the conventions of textual encoding for the purposes of onscreen publication.

There are times when doing it right from the outset makes more sense. In particular I would warn potential project managers about the hazards of OCR (Optical Character Recognition) scanning. With one source for the *Lear* Archive I scanned material from a printed edition. While it worked for quite a bit of the text, the OCR programme, like Word, is given to making educated guesses when it does not recognise a word. As a result, for Henry Irving I was given, with no great consistency, either Icing or driving. After years of proof-reading this text I am still finding scanning errors (for example an r and n for m, which is very difficult to catch on screen). If I had it to do again I think I might well opt to retype the material rather than scan it into digital form (Fig. 6).

3.2. Software limitations

With the CUP Archive we were restricted from the outset by the publishing software which the Press have licensed, Dynatext. This package is very sophisticated in its handling of text but, as we discovered, has much more trouble dealing with images. This problem has been tackled by adding a special browser to the already existing package specifically for viewing the image database. Having the Press as a publisher has therefore both presented the restriction of using a specific publishing package which I did not chose and the advantage of having the skills of programmers who could adapt that package to suit the needs of this particular project. In general, using already available software is far simpler and much less expensive and time consuming than creating your own. Most packages offer quite a bit of flexibility and can be quite user-friendly, but the assistance of technical experts is still often required. Make sure that your budget allows for the employment of technical expertise at this stage if you do not possess it yourself.

Another general rule is that using standard file formats and mark-up languages saves time, provides compatibility and often provides you with a built in help network online. The Dynatext software required that I use SGML (Standard Generalized Markup Language) and therefore I was both helped and restricted by the double-edged sword which standards of this kind offer. On the one hand, courses offered to instruct me in this language were widely available. On the other hand, because the kinds of links and the number of links we wanted to use surpassed anything Cambridge had ever done before, there was a great deal of trial and error on both my part and the part of Peter Robinson, CUP's computer consultant and advisor on the project. The Finder Text in particular has posed problems because I wanted to create both an edition of sorts, which requires careful attention to layout as well as functionality, and an archive of both text and images which is searchable.

Along with copyright restrictions, software limitations can force changes in the project which you would rather not make. Again it is important to approach each limitation as an opportunity to improve the original design concept. If the software does not do what you want,

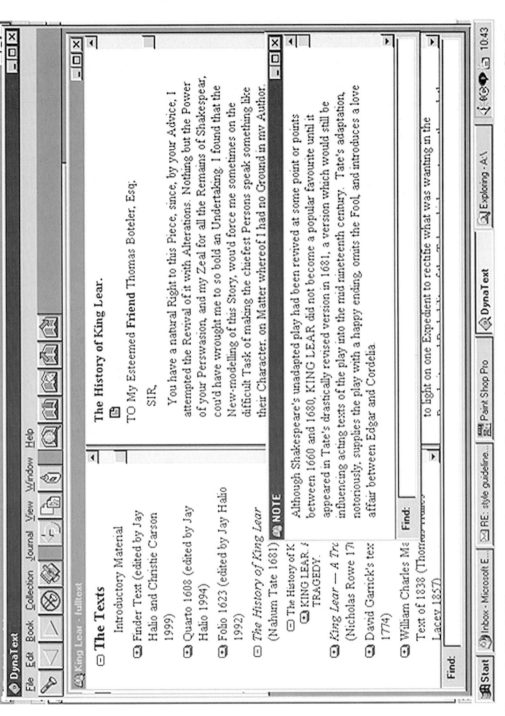

Figure 6: The full Tate text and four other edited and acting editions of the play are available in full on the CD. These texts have been licensed from Chadwyck-Healey Ltd and reproduced with the permission of Cambridge University Press

does it do something which might be comparable or which will achieve the same effect in the long run? At each stage it is important to reassess the individual choices insofar as they affect the overall objectives of the project as a whole. If at any point you find yourself being drawn away from your original intent it is essential that you feel comfortable with that decision. Revisiting your choices again and again can, in fact, act to strengthen and focus your original concept.

4. POST-PRODUCTION

One of the most frustrating aspects of creating projects of this kind is trying to take them through the conventional processes of editing and proof-reading. If the project has succeeded in being truly non-linear, it will be essential to test not only every link but every pathway through the material to ensure it works properly. If you decide to make changes at this stage these changes can have knock-on effects. The result is that at each prototype stage, proof-reading must begin again. Be warned, as a result of these difficulties we are working on our *tenth* prototype for the *Lear* CD.

4.1. Testing and feedback

In an ideal world the best possible way to refine and improve your project at this point is to go through a series of user tests and feedback sessions. Users who do not know the material well will quickly discover mistakes and anomalies. Consistency of approach, or lack of it, will be picked up in sessions of this sort. With the *Lear* CD I have taken a number of opportunities to present the prototype at conferences. The responses of colleagues have been extremely productive and have added to the complexity and completeness of the final project.

At this final stage it is necessary to step back from the project and try to see it through the eyes of a first-time user. The process of going through the project with unfamiliar users will help also to create support materials which will enhance the users' enjoyment of the material. The work put in at this stage will increase the professionalism of the final project and will ensure that, once your work is finally made available, it is friendly and helpful for the user.

4.2. Publication

The final stage in the entire process is, of course, publication in whatever form you have chosen. With publication, even if this just means posting the project on a local web server, another issue arises and that is ongoing user support. Support is an issue which you must think through at the outset of a project but finalise at this point. If the users have questions where can they go? How much time and energy after the completion of the project are you willing to put in? One of the great challenges of working in this area is the fact that the project may never be completed in the sense that a book is when it goes to print. From the users' point of view this is a great advantage. From your point of view it may be one of the greatest drawbacks of engaging in this arena. It is something to consider. For you as project manager, when does your responsibility stop?

5. CONCLUSIONS

The field of digital resource creation is very new. Theatrical digital resources are particularly few and far between. As a pioneer of sorts in this area I am of the opinion that I carry a fair degree of responsibility. In specific terms, with regards to the *Lear* Archive I feel a sense of responsibility to the current and past scholars whose work is included, to ensure that their work is adequately represented. There is a responsibility to the creative artists whose work is displayed, both in terms of correctly crediting that work and paying for it. Finally, there is the responsibility of making sure that the intellectual framework used to support the digital project as a whole is both challenging and transparent. Often scholarship of one era has discredited, discounted or erased the scholarship of its predecessors. This kind of thinking assumes a progression of thought similar to the evangelical technological determinism which has now also been discredited. In order to learn from the scholars who have gone before it is necessary to present their work in an even-handed fashion which allows current researchers to make up their own minds about the validity of the approach taken.

What is exciting about digital technology is its capacity to show the history of scholarship, the history of a canonical text and even the history of the process of canon creation. Because of my belief in the responsibility involved in this work I support the creation of contained edited packages of information. Rather than depending on the World Wide Web to provide us with all the information we might ever need in a random and uncredited way, I am increasingly convinced that carefully selected and linked materials will prove valuable to future scholars and students.

5.1. Strengths and weaknesses of the *Lear* CD

To look finally at the advantages and disadvantages of the CD I have created I would say that, on balance, it will prove to be a valuable resource. It has the advantages of collecting together previously unconnected and geographically disparate materials. It has the advantage of drawing together the strengths of the approaches presented by performance and textual studies scholarship. It has the advantage over print media of having a series of digital texts which can be searched, compared and linked to additional information: the large database of photographs, if printed in book form, could not be reorganised to appear repeatedly in different orders and contexts. The ability to search the archive to access information about particular actors, characters, productions, etc. gives this project a huge advantage over the collection of similar materials in a less dynamic medium.

There are a number of limitations to the project as well which I am happy to acknowledge as they form the basis of my new explorations in the area of digital media and its application to theatre studies. The first is the lack of sound and images. While I am still not convinced that the materials which are currently available for transfer to this medium would have been suitable for inclusion in this particular project, I am increasingly convinced that new materials created with this medium in mind could greatly enhance the study of performance. At one stage we considered the possibility of video-taping actors performing various textual variations of certain key scenes. This idea proved too expensive and unwieldy but I do believe it still has potential.

Another great limitation of the CD as it currently exists is its very limited ability to address the temporal and spatial elements of performance. While I have arranged material so that it forms two separate timelines, this is a false imposition on a format which is not comfortable with this kind of display. I would have been happier with a graphic timeline rather than a textual one. At one time I envisioned a map which could illustrate the spread of performances of the play as it moved out from London at the centre. This graphic demonstration would have been able to illustrate a great deal about colonial patterns as well as stage history but again, alas, it was deemed too difficult. The interface which we were faced with is utilitarian but I would very much have liked to work with a graphic designer to develop an interface that was more user-friendly in a number of ways.

Finally, the most glaring limitation of this project is the fact that it will quickly be out of date. The fact that it is being produced as a CD means that updates are not possible unless a new edition of the CD is produced. From my point of view as project manager this is a blessed relief. For users, however, I can see that the material will quickly be dated.

5.2. Future plans

As a result of the frustrations I describe I have involved myself in two new projects which I hope will allow me to address some of these issues. The first is entitled *Three Lears*, a project headed up by the theatre designer, Chris Dyer, who has recently joined the staff at Royal Holloway. This project will involve the creation of 3D models of three of his own designs of the play, each of which was created for a very different theatre space: a thrust stage at the Stratford Festival Ontario, the black box theatre at the Other Place for the RSC and the proscenium arch theatre at the Theatre Royal in Glasgow. To these spatial models of the space will be attached research materials about the productions in question. This project will attempt to add a spatial element to the interface between the researcher and the performance history material. The project will also be able to address the differences between the various theatre spaces through the production of a single play at a specific time.

The second project, which I will lead, is a design archive of Shakespearean performance in London and Stratford-upon-Avon between 1960 and 2000. Again it will be an archive but the emphasis will be on the visual and spatial aspects of production rather than the text. A database of production credits for the whole period will be supported by production photographs, 3D models of designs and video interviews with the participating actors, directors and designers. The aim of these two new projects will be then to focus on the aspects of multimedia technology which might prove the most useful in support of theatre research.

Theatre research has been limited severely by the limited ephemera which has been available to represent performance. I would like to encourage a new approach to the archiving of theatrical materials. Multimedia technology allows for access to the bulky and delicate research materials which previously have been unavailable or which have had limited access, like costumes, sets, costume designs, programmes and props. Digital video opens the possibility of real time and recorded contact with the creators of theatre. In the long run, as theatres take up digital means of creation themselves it will be increasingly easy to make those materials available to a wider audience. A digital promptbook used by a professional theatre could be copied and distributed to universities and theatre schools. The quantity and quality of material available to study theatre may well increase exponentially over the coming years. It is for this reason that it is important to take a long hard look at the intellectual frameworks which we are putting in place to deal with this information.

5.3. Final thoughts

While I would not want the *Lear* CD to be seen as definitive or representative in any way, I also accept the responsibility which comes with working in a new area. Given that there are so few projects of this kind currently available it may well become a groundbreaking and therefore ground-determining piece of work by default. It is for this reason that I have tried to make the *Lear* Archive for CUP as consistent in its intellectual approach as possible. It is also for this reason that for my next two projects I would like to tackle very different aspects of the idea of archiving theatrical materials using multimedia technology. Hypertext is a powerful means of creating and recreating meaning. I would like to see, however, if there are other ways of interfacing with information of this kind.

The theatre uses so many senses and I would very much like to explore methods of study which tap into those senses as well. Meaning can be created spatially and visually through proximity. I would like to see a great deal more investigation of these spatial and visual kinds of languages and their usefulness in the area of digital theatre research. Thus, despite the trials of the process I describe I have not been dissuaded from my original conviction that digital resources have the potential to change the face of theatre research radically. I hope that I have also not discouraged potential new project managers from making their own discoveries in this exciting new field. It has been a difficult but rewarding journey.

2.3: Approaches to building digital archives
by Barry Smith

1. ORIGINS

'Mummy, Mummy, where do digital archives come from?'

I've never been asked this question and, come to think about it, probably never will. But it's the nub of an interesting question just the same and an essential one if you're thinking of starting to 'digitally archive' something. Given that the word 'archive' derives from the Greek 'arkheia' meaning 'public records', it's small wonder the word usually describes, or described, local, regional and national government collections of documents and other records kept for consultation and research purposes (contemporary ones sometimes with an embargo prohibiting access before a given date, presumably to protect the guilty). Frequently such public archives have been complemented (occasionally contradicted) by private collections of letters, diaries and notes (military and scientific collections being foremost in this category though literary papers have latterly achieved increasing significance too). We can note in passing – and perhaps as a spur to start one! – that theatre collections can prove valuable: the British Library has recently paid £1.2 million to buy for the nation the vast collection of private papers, letters, photographs and diaries of the late Laurence Olivier. We can also note that Amazon.co.uk currently rank Olivier's *Henry V* (1945) at number 53 in the Sales List of most popular DVDs: digital resources have indeed entered the marketplace!

Even in such a brief overview one can sense new digital facilities making their presence felt. It's a passing thought that in the past the sheer welter of paper in government administration (letters, minutes and internal memorandum) ensured the longevity of ideas and discussions and strategies as they were bundled off, literally tied up with red tape, to the Records Office. Now, the advent of gov.uk (equivalent of ac.uk in government) means an increasing amount of discussion and conferencing is undertaken in the far less permanent medium of e-mail. In the arts too the impact of 'the digital' is now acknowledged without necessarily full cognisance of what is or will be involved, as the call for papers for the CADE 2001 [Computers in Art & Design] Conference makes clear:

> Most practitioners and educationists in art and design now acknowledge the wide-ranging impact of digital media, even though they may not yet recognise the character of its potential nor how to engage with it.
> [from an e-mail circulated on many Mailbase Lists, 17 June 2000.]

Just as word-processing was one of the first useful digital applications for many areas of study

– not least the performing arts – so the 'digital archive' in various forms is proving to be one of the most widespread subsequent applications. Imperative in any archive – whether public or private, paper or digital – is the primary 'documentation' (primarily but no longer as necessarily paper-based as the word 'document' suggests), and the notion of a collection or accumulation of related items which are in part at least systematised or ordered or, in modern parlance, searchable. Because the 'digital archive' concept is very recent, it still usually involves recording, cataloguing or sometimes replicating paper-based documentation, but it is unlikely to continue in this way and indeed already it is changing. There are already 'archives' which exist *solely* in digital form, particularly e-mail. For instance, all JISCMail Lists (the UK e-mail correspondence facility for subject groups in Higher Education – funded, monitored and maintained by the UK's Higher Education Funding Councils). JISCMail Lists are automatically archived for a period of two years then deleted unless a special case is made for retention. But some Lists have made a much greater feature of longevity, creating named archives by requesting subscribers to send in their contributions, ideas, essays and 'papers' for permanent digital archiving – and thus creating a permanent 'digital archive' seemingly out of nothing.

Fans of Richard Brautigan may feel this is nothing new. In his novel *The Abortion: An Historical Romance* (1996) Brautigan created the magnificent if impractical notion of a huge underground library/archive for all the *unpublished* manuscript novels in the world – so that all and any rejected novels could find a resting place and be salvageable. Fans duly tried to create such a facility in Burlington, Vermont, USA, and an archive of donated manuscripts does exist at the Burlington Fletcher Free Library (but rapidly became so over-subscribed that it is sadly no longer able to accept new submissions!). The problem can be digitally solved in an instant, of course, and has been. There is now a digital-only Brautigan Virtual Library where you can submit your unpublished novel which qualifies you to read all or any of the others. There is also, inevitably, a Brautigan Mailing List devoted to correspondence about the author, a Traders' Corner (memorabilia, signed copies etc.), bibliography and links pages, the totality making a (perhaps 'a' rather than 'the', for there are several other related collections on the Internet) Brautigan Archive. This easy networking of both large and small collections and associated interests is becoming a key aspect of digital archives on the Internet. As yet at a very early stage and still in a confused state, the links facilitated by any hypertexted document or database means that new, well-organised additions can quickly find their rightful place in the collections of information and data about any chosen subject.

One of the earliest digital-only archives was a Usenet newsgroup called *Talk.origins* devoted to mainstream theories in geology, biology, cosmology and theology. Contributions essentially arguing the Darwinian evolutionary line were posted and, though often sent anonymously, seemed to bear all the hallmarks of serious research, close argument and bibliographic referencing. It inevitably attracted the attention of the Creationists who after some predictable hubris set up their own equivalent e-mail archive rather wittily named *True.origins*. These two archives still exist and expand side by side in an uneasy truce, reflecting not only the ability of the Net and digital facility to create archives of some seriousness and substance apparently from thin air but also, with contributions from a Professor_Enigma@hotmail.com for example, to maintain that anonymity and game-playing which is such a basic ingredient of the Internet. Not that vast tracts of serious thought are beyond reach either. The 'History of Thought Archive' at McMaster University, mirrored in the UK at Bristol University, in Australia at Melbourne University and with the Université de Paris, Sorbonne, adding a French 'Bibliothèque

Virtuelle', is, through the means of a relatively simple international collaboration, building a digital archive on its chosen specialism of the History of Economics. It does this through the simple expedient of reproducing essential philosophical essays (with permission or those out of copyright restrictions) relating to the topic and inviting all interested participants to contribute to its moderated but burgeoning bibliography. In networked digital archives this emergence of an interactive user/contributor axis is a very noticeable and intriguing feature.

If you search systematically on the Net you are most likely to find an 'archive' with some reference to your point of interest. This might be anything from the Searchable Online Archive of Recipes at Berkeley (67,087 recipes to date) to the Mechanical Music Digest Compilation Archive (on musical instruments which play themselves) which seems to average an incredible additional 14 contributions of knowledge, opinion and insight per day. Google Search returns nearly 3 million archive references, AltaVista, with its looser approach to indexing, over 14 million, both of which only represent a fraction of the totality. The largest Net Archive that I am personally aware of is called 'Internet Archives' which, as of March 2000, claimed one billion pages, fifty thousand FTP sites, sixteen million relevant postings and is the equivalent of about a thousand complete copies of *Encyclopaedia Britannica*. Started in 1996 it still welcomes donations of data and claims to grow in size by 10% a month. Its reputation as 'the biggest' may not last as rumours persist that some wag is about to launch 'The Archive of Everything'! In sharp contrast, at least in scale, 'personal archives' seem to be a rapidly increasing feature of the Net too, where individuals and families trace their genealogy by researching parish registers, posting family photographs and other memorabilia, inviting others to contribute additional pieces to the jigsaw. Once more the user/contributor axis is in evidence.

That developing an archive or database on the Internet can still be the territory of the novice should not mask the fact that professionalisation and (relative) standardisation have continued apace, none more so than by the professional librarians and archivists of UK Government and Higher Education who have made enormous and worthwhile inroads into and contributions to the so-called Information Society. Indeed, in many respects they are creating the Information Society. Their task is, to say the least, daunting; vast collections, in some instances accumulated over centuries – sometimes of enormous intrinsic and extrinsic value and totally unique – suddenly needing to be available in some digital indexed format. A recent announcement from the Cabinet Office that it is to set up a consortium consisting of the Public Record Office, the British Library and the Royal Commission on Historical Manuscripts, with support from the National Council on Archives, the Society of Archivists and the Association of Chief Archivists in Local Government gives a glimpse into the sheer scale and professionalism of the task and the seriousness which it is afforded. And 'afforded' is a term of some consequence where the investment necessary is usually measured in at least large fractions of a million pounds sterling and sometimes significantly more. The development of accessible digital archives for future generations is a serious business.

If, when you contemplate this maelstrom of new digital applications, you still feel some urge to jump in but are not sure quite how to or what you should be clutching as you leap, the 'personal archive' is perhaps the easiest point of entry. Not that I particularly want to encourage everyone to be posting pictures of great-grandmother. My recommendation would be more along the lines of the Brautigan hypothesis that everyone can write at least one (unpublished) novel, that there is a place for the willing beginner to indulge their specialist knowledge and make it available to others. Collaboration with another or others with identical, similar or related interests can be a key ingredient in developing useful collections from such relatively small beginnings and the advent of e-mail makes it relatively easy to locate those persons through Lists, UseNet newsgroups and even Chat Lines. The naturally unwary should perhaps be reminded that the Internet inevitably contains many jokers, games and absurdities and that archive-building and database development have significantly changed and become more professional in very recent years. However the essential ingredients remain an over-riding interest in the material or idea/notion to be archived or databased, a modicum of time in the early stages to get to grips with the major pitfalls and advantages of the activity and the confidence to ask for assistance occasionally. With those three ingredients the rest is relatively easy.

2. GETTING HELP

As standards and technical complexities have increased so, fortunately, have the various help facilities supporting them. In Higher Education this is a central concern of the AHDS (Arts and Humanities Data Service) and its subgroups including, for the performing arts, PADS (Performing Arts Data Service) and the visual arts, VADS (Visual Arts Data Service). One specific role of PADS and VADS is to act as a bridge between the initial enquiry and the resulting digital works and they are also equipped to act as a possible depository for final outcomes. For both the novice and the more experienced, one or both of them should be listed as a first port of call.

The importance of seeking collaboration and asking for assistance should not be under-estimated. It is difficult to build a digital database single-handed without some recourse to advanced technical expertise at some juncture or without some assistance with data-input. And it is equally unwise to set about building either a database or an archive without recourse to at least a second opinion, some user-testing procedures and a check that the software you propose to use meets the increasingly stringent national and international standards. But for the relative or total novice there are enormous resources of friendly information freely available on all aspects of archiving and databases from colleagues already working the field. The generous spirit of the early e-mail communities is today perhaps sometimes hedged with concerns about the sheer overload of e-mail and Lists, but it still generally exists within specific HE e-mail communities (and interestingly enough on most Chat Lines, where information and guidance on the latest technological developments tends to be freely discussed if sometimes in a disarmingly frank manner!). Higher Education Lists (previously hosted by Mailbase and from 1st August 2000 by JISCmail at the CLRC) provide an extraordinary assortment of freely available lines of enquiry and one can pick carefully for the one or two that sound the most pertinent. Small wonder, given the Library and Information Services emphasis on digitising activities, that Library Lists form one of the largest collections of Lists on JISCmail (over 220 in all; you are advised not to try joining all of them nor even the 23 specifically devoted to electronic resources). Other Lists with electronic aspects as a focal point currently offer a choice of 95 Lists (including AHDS and PADS as noted above), a further 16 on Archives and a further 28 with databases on subjects as varied as fish and Robert Graves (that's two separate databases not one). Given this overwhelming wealth of potential information and help sources, the greatest difficulty is probably in choosing one. They can all be found via http://jiscmail.ac.uk/

Even if you initially choose the wrong one, someone will more than likely suggest an adviser for your particular problem, however basic. If still in doubt and your subject matter is related to performing arts, choose PADS.

3. THE LIVE ART ARCHIVE

As one of the earliest Internet arts databases the Live Art Archive is situated between the two extremes of the wholly paper-based set of records and the wholly digital: in this it is a product of its time (mid 1990s) and now shows both the best and worst features of the technology that was then current. I have told the story of its cardboard box origins many times, mostly at conferences as a spur to others to see what lurks in their cupboards or under their desks, but will repeat it briefly one more time as a declaration to readers that they can easily do it too. And then lay it to rest.

In 1978 I found myself running a small performance 'black box' venue in Nottingham. Arrangements were amazingly informal (for example entrance was free!) During the 1980s the touring programme, the venue administration and the touring companies became much more 'professional' in their dealings and, perhaps most significantly of all, pricing was introduced. Suddenly we were in the business of 'advance programming' and with that went selection. As that happened, and with a natural student audience primarily interested in new work plus staff interests in 'live art' and 'performance art', we found ourselves with a key venue and a flood of interest in a particular area of new work. This flood appeared mainly in the form of mail from small companies and individuals requesting an opportunity to show their work: as venues and arts organisations had 'professionalised' so had the performance companies. Sometimes this mail was simply a letter, more often than not it contained a specimen handbill, perhaps a poster or review of a previous event. The amount of this material was overwhelming – several packets on any one working day was standard – and particularly given that at best we could only hope to programme twelve (cheaper) events a year, the quantity of it was a little daunting. What would these days be called 'an effective management strategy' was a cardboard box under the desk. When that box was full I found another box. Eventually I couldn't get any more boxes under the desk and resisting cries of 'Chuck 'Em Away' moved them to a cupboard. Even then my reasoning wasn't remotely connected to archiving but I was aware that the boxes had acquired a useful function: students pursuing some line of enquiry on their contemporary performance role models could happily rummage through the boxes in search of bits of information. Years later I cringe at the information which must have met its end scissored into student essays but it seemed a good idea at the time.

The new all-the-rage Loco Script – an apparently intelligent word-processor – provided the next stage. It had a facility which could 'instantly' find words in a text on one of its memory files no matter how long (within reason) the document. If the word 'Impact' for example (as in 'Impact Theatre Cooperative') was entered, it would highlight every time that word occurred (whether the company name or someone else claiming 'impact' in their show). Despite its limitations it seemed quite magical, promising almost instant identification of which box of jumble the sought-after details might be located. It also offered instant accessing of detailed information. The first attempt I laboriously undertook was an edition of 'Performance Magazine' – it took literally days to enter the information but at the end of the process one of sixty-four editions was fully indexed and offered the seemingly magical facility of instant recall of any item.

The ordering of this jumble of information had a similarly unlikely start. In 1983 a new technician, John Dyper, registered for part-time studies in History and Anthropology and encountered e-mail. As a result, he constantly demonstrated (in the form of a hideously unattractive screen full of gobbledygook with some sort of friendly human response buried in the middle of it) to anyone who would listen the magic of how a question sent out in the evening could result in 20+ answers from all around the world by the following morning. It seemed extraordinary. Moreover these responses sometimes seemed aware of indexes and 'databases' that other individuals in the field were developing which promised access to information never before so freely available, probably never before conceived.

Two other key individuals entered the fray: Sally Phillips who was a trained secretary with fast typing speeds, skilled in the new attributes of word-processing and interested in the content of those boxes, and Anthony Jordan, a new member of staff in University Computing Services who constantly talked up something called 'micro-systems' and, wonder of wonders, actually seemed able to come up with trial versions on screen of what you could only half-imagine in your mind's eye as a silver dream racing machine. These represent the key individuals and essential attributes needed to start any database/archive: enthusiasm, technical competence and data input/management. Whereas it had taken me several painstaking evenings to index one slim volume, Sally could rattle through pages with extraordinary dexterity and accuracy; whereas a list was the best that could formerly be achieved now it was multi-faceted, data divided between different 'fields' that could be separately interrogated and would yield answers instantly. And, best of all, data could be added piecemeal and the database would sort it appropriately. Now, 200,000 items of information later, practitioners are amazed at the detailed collation. 'Argh! My whole life is flashing before me!' said a recent user – but we had never collected his works in any organised or structured sense, only piecemeal over several years. Asked to extricate just his work (for the first time) the database did just that and ordered it sequentially. The longer-term effect of a steady accretion of information to a database – a genuine pooling of knowledge – has to be seen to be believed.

Although collaboration is essential it will inevitably lead to some compromises by all parties. A more positive way of looking at it is that the collaboration is a small 'focus group' which can determine the best possible solution in the circumstances to reach the desired objective. If you have four people in a room discussing how a new database might work it is likely that you will have four databases on the drawing board: different people will think different aspects are important. As both a web site and a database inevitably rely on an hierarchical structure to a certain extent (however much general free-text search facilities may ameliorate this situation) a firm final decision is essential. It may be as simple a problem as 'What word/words appear at the top of the web site page as it downloads?' or as difficult a problem as 'What fields are we going to offer users?' As soon as you determine any category you are likely to find an example that doesn't quite fit! Frustrating though that may be, it is best seen as a valuable part of the exercise and it is far better to talk through these difficult cases and reach a firm rationalised decision which henceforth can assume the status of 'policy' than fudge the issue which will leave subsequent users confused. This is particularly important if the project is of a sufficient scale to lead to data processing and input being undertaken by hired staff rather than the originators and creators.

4. SEARCHING

Central to any database facility is the effectiveness of its search facility. It is essential at the outset to think through what the database will be used for. There is inevitably a temptation to develop it so that it is useful for the developer, to support his/her range of interests. It is essential, however, to think wider than this – even perhaps forming 'focus groups' or inviting others to comment on the effectiveness of trial runs – because other potential users reveal likely demands, attitudes and lines of enquiry which it is doubtful if not impossible for one person to originate. The student, the critic, the practitioner, the general reader, the nerd and the novice will all have quite different expectations of what a database should provide and how it will provide it. Although it may not be possible to satisfy all groups it is better knowingly *not* to cover a particular feature than realise later that you haven't covered it.

We have consistently followed the so-called '3 Cs' of any contemporary collection: Complete, Current and Correct. That is the standard we aim for, not necessarily the one yet achieved! As well as saving all likely sources for entry at the first opportunity, the Live Art Archive, in order at least to approach *completion,* has visited practitioners' private collections, checked archived details with practitioners at all available opportunities and, more recently, in a very restricted number of cases, designed specific practitioner web sites to encourage a range of new information, illustration and reviews. The problem of *currency* is less difficult once all known lines of communication (circulars, listings etc.) have been systemised. Even then *correctness* may prove problematic and one of our greatest hazards is a performance that is widely advertised but for one reason or another doesn't happen. In the recent case of Kira O'Reilly – whose performance eventually *didn't* take place in the expected format owing to Health and Safety requirements (23rd March 2000) – we could hardly miss knowing about it as we were uncomfortably close to the centre of the storm of debate about freedom of the artist. But that need not always be the case. In this particular instance we archived the fierce debate and final outcome though it did feel slightly odd to have archived an event which didn't happen! From the sublime to the cor-blimey, any database entry relies on perfect spelling so proof-reading and cross-checking becomes an essential aspect of the job.

There was one final 'big decision' to make in 1994 once a sizeable collection of data had been amassed, which will still face the contemporary collector – to make the information available via the (then equally new-fangled) Internet or on a CD-ROM? It was not a decision that took any time at all and still doesn't: if the collection is no longer on-going, if it has reached an appropriate plateau of those 3 Cs – complete, current and correct – then the CD-ROM (or more likely currently the DVD) offers the perfect solution. But if one of more of those is still 'work in progress', the Internet database offers the better solution as it can be constantly updated and provide instant new information. We still update the Live Art Archive weekly and will continue to do so for the foreseeable future.

5. MAINTENANCE

That, however, raises one further important issue that it is imperative for the private or lone archive developer to take cognisance of early in the development period – how is the archive to be *maintained* (which immediately has knock-on revenue costs in terms of staffing, accommodation, equipment, back-up and security, migration of data costs as technology develops); and how *ended*? It is wise from the outset to build in an 'exit strategy' (other than bankruptcy or death). An exit strategy should be time-based – either the subject or the research period being defined by strict dates – or, more difficult, implemented when a pre-determined level of thoroughness has been achieved. The worst exit strategy is to keep on going until the money and/or energy runs out, whereupon edges will appear frayed (all too apparent on an un-maintained web site), and a degree of decay will become evident to the user. Both eventualities are certain unless a strategy is planned.

The central service offered by any database is inevitably going to be its search facility; see, for example, search: http://art.ntu.ac.uk/liveart/lasearch.htm.
This will be the core feature assisted by a range of additional information; user guidance, help features etc. In this instance we chose the following:

- e-mail: an auto-addressed live link for enquiries;

- an alphabetical index listing all facilities for easier location:
  index: http://art.ntu.ac.uk/liveart/subindex.htm;

- a supporting (Mailbase) List with easy links to join:
  letters: http://art.ntu.ac.uk/liveart/letters.htm;

- basic information covering origins, personnel, copyright statements etc., information:
  http://art.ntu.ac.uk/liveart/database.htm;

- a facility for users to add data (which would be checked before inclusion in the database):
  add data: http://art.ntu.ac.uk/liveart/adddata.htm;

- and of course Links to associated web sites:
  links: http://art.ntu.ac.uk/liveart/links.htm.

The Links feature begins to build *the* archive by inter-linking several sources. But two words of warning: recognise that Links will, in normal circumstances, take people away from your facility; and be aware as you make those Links that they will quickly expand and need sub-categorisation, constant updating and exhaustive maintenance. There is software available (such as WebCoaster) that will check your Links and report if a problem is encountered but it will still require an intervention to correct the Links List and add new sites. The contemporary answer seems to be to be highly selective in the Links you offer, determine the sub-categories you intend to array them in and stick to those. Five years ago we determined ten categories relevant to the concerns of the Live Art Archive (which, on reflection, was probably too many but we were early in the field and inexperienced); having chosen them we have maintained them. Hopefully self-explanatory and as directly relevant to Live Art concerns as possible, they are:

(see http://art.ntu.ac.uk/liveart/links.htm)
- Other Related Archives
- Practitioners
- Venues
- Opportunities and Events
- Documentation of Past Events

- Arts Courses
- Bibliography
- E-mail Lists and E-zines
- Search Engines and Directories
- Miscellaneous

Finally, register your archive/database wherever possible. The first place I registered with was the Higher Education Database List (now defunct) that at that time consisted of only seven databases, all seven being Chemical Compounds... I was making a point! The more places you register the more likelihood that Search Engines will locate your site (you can register with the main ones directly but there are in fact hundreds of different ones) and the domino effect will start. It can be instructive to imagine yourself as a potential user using basic search terms and try to locate yourself on standard Search Engines – on one you may be listed amongst the first ten or twenty, or even top: on others you may find your site isn't listed at all. That's the one to register on!

6. CONCLUSIONS

I have related the background and structure of The Live Art Archive in some detail because its origins and shape still reveal a pattern that any new archive might essentially follow. But what is collected, by what means, and how it is stored – in a word, 'software' – is rapidly developing: in particular the collation of still and moving images and sound files. Technological developments offer new opportunities and this is the case with the most recent archive currently under development alongside The Live Art Archive: The Digital Performance Archive. This archive (arising from an AHRB project in collaboration with Steve Dixon and The University of Salford) is dedicated to capturing and documenting developments in the creative use of computer technologies in performance 1999–2000 and their antecedents. It is partly dependent upon collating extant paper-based documentation but, much more significantly, is archiving events which have only ever occurred in a digital format (for example cyberspace interactive dramas, webcast performances etc.). This requires capture ('cloning') of web sites and documentation of resulting live events. There is a new emphasis upon – and technical capability to realise – storage of still and moving images way beyond the capabilities of the software available in the mid 1990s. And this, in terms of software, is where a database for a contemporary archive needs to begin.

This being the case, by way of conclusion I am therefore briefly listing the technical details of the *new* database (as described by the University's Senior IT Technician, Mr Stuart Moore, who has developed it). Many readers might see this moment as an opportunity to practice 'the glaze technique' mentioned in the Introduction but two other general conclusions may also be drawn: firstly that development of software moves on quickly and remorselessly and it is essential to commence with the most current version available; secondly that its satisfactory manipulation to achieve the desired end-result requires technical expertise within creative team-working. This, fortunately, is unlikely to be strange territory to anyone who has ever undertaken directing a performance event. When the relationship between those two factors is right, that's where digital archives come from!

The Digital Performance Archive
Technical Description

The DPA archive is based on a MySQL database, accessed through a number of PHP3 scripts. This is all hosted on an NT Server running IIS4.0 which actually serves up the data. The machine hosting all this is a PIII 450 with 256Mb of memory and 70Gb of RAID5 storage.

All administration of the site is carried out through web pages so that the data can be altered from any location providing username/password are authorised.

The decision to use MySQL (http://www.mysql.org) was based on its cost (free for educational usage) and the speed of operation on smaller size databases. The only feature missing which could have come in useful is transactional control; however this limitation has been overcome through coding within the php scripts.

The database has been quite heavily normalised to allow for easy updating and the fluid nature of the data it contains. Also, due to the use of ANSI SQL, we have a database which can, with minimal fuss, be moved between platforms should the need arise for different features.

PHP (http://www.php.net) was used for the scripting because of its high level of support for MySQL functions, and speed. Currently PHP3 is being used; however a move to PHP4 is planned which should bring another increase of speed due to being able to implement the PHP execution as a dll call, rather than as a call to an external cgi program.

Currently the database is performing well, with most searches being returned in under a second, and preliminary tests have shown that this should scale well with increased usage.

Stuart Moore, Senior IT Technician

2.4: Scholarly Skywriting: *Sound Journal* and other projects
by Alan Beck

My title is borrowed from Steve Harnad (Harnad 1999), with thanks. He championed those peer-reviewed Internet journals which are free-to-view and independent of commercial publishers. And he argued that scholarly articles made available on the web are 'like a piece of skywriting, visible to one and all, today and forever more'. The ability to self-publish, as a group of peer-reviewing scholars, is with us *now*. Copyright remains with the authors and, all in all, this is a revolution for research. I describe below how I set up *Sound Journal* along with a couple of other projects and, hopefully, I encourage others to go and do likewise. First, I deal with the nuts and bolts of design and then I consider three interleaved issues – copyright, promoting the journal and opposition to electronic publishing. I also question why so many e-journals look formal and 'printy', mimicking the paper-based model when all e-journals can enjoy the value-added features of the Net: faster publication, multimedia, decreased costs, archiving, more collaborative work, data sharing and energising the key tasks of publishing research – quality control, dissemination, peer dialogue.

1. SETTING UP *SOUND JOURNAL*

Assisted by a peer-review panel, I set up *Sound Journal* in 1998, along with co-editor Dave Reason, Senior Lecturer in Image Studies. We are skywriters, building what we hope is a journal of high-quality scholarship. Our mission in going online is to be innovative, to gain global accessibility and internationalism in research along with rapid updating and interaction with readers. Not being burdened with subscriptions or shipping, the group's focus, along with that of our audience and potential contributors, is the value of scholarship in itself, its reliability, new-style electronic layout and consistency into the future. *Sound Journal* also led me to undertake other web projects and they too will be briefly mentioned below: an e-supplement to *Studies in Theatre Production* [*STP*] and a Radio Theory Site. Such developments augment my university courses which are 'paperless'; the departmental Intranet supplying a range of materials and all the organisation along with links to the web enlivened with images, sound files, varying designs, little self-tests and speedy navigation aids.

The *Sound Journal* is available at http://www.ukc.ac.uk/sdfva/sound-journal/.
An alternative in print was not financially feasible. We would be an 'independent' (no-cost, non-trade, and what is termed 'esoteric', that is, for a specialist audience). Immediately I encountered opinions against e-publishing and a reactionary disdain for the web. Opposing

voices said things like: 'I would never publish on the web' or 'I'll be plagiarised' or 'A virtual journal is too virtual for me' or 'The Internet is full of here-today-and-gone-tomorrow'. Such anti-web sentiments have been interestingly surveyed, at least among German scholars in Canada, by Warkentin (1997) and he found that 42% in this very traditional area refused to publish digitally. Even today I meet the rare academic at theatre gatherings of UK drama departments who says 'My college hasn't supplied me with a desktop computer'. We need more research on this and recommendations by professional associations on the minimum electronic support a department should give a teacher. I suggest they should be read alongside Mark Batty's essential *Very Basic Introduction to IT*.

It is a different matter if a scholar says to me – and one or two have – 'I will not publish in your journal' if what is at issue is the quality of *Sound Journal* in itself. *Sound Journal* is now finding its place in the academic community but the road so far has been challenging and, I will confess, a couple of mistakes have been made. The founding concept had a single focus – sound – but 'sound' across disciplines, from drama, film and radio to music, anthropology and psychoanalysis. Part of the struggle is that it is tied to emerging research areas – radio studies, the film sound track and the aesthetics of sound in performance. It also attempts to straddle current research boundaries and to bring together a number of what are called 'invisible colleges'.

We started in an initial burst of techno-optimism. Dave and I intended to ask the panel, contributors and readers to 'think electronic' rather than 'think print'. Like most good ideas this was easy to understand and tough to realise. Explorers on a new scholarly frontier in 1996–7, we surfed for other e-journals and quickly discovered the hits and pits in terms of design. Some offered a studied 'grunge' look, perhaps as a guarantee of their respectability. Others were out-and-out 'printy', mimicking the appearance and feel of paper-based journals (see Smith 1999a). A rare few seductively played with postmodernist style, typically in cinematics or gender. Then there was another puzzle: in what format should we publish? Was it to be HTML or PDF or SGML? PDF was rejected as being too uncomfortably 'printy' and too restrictive for our multimedia future. We also wanted a fully paperless publishing cycle from writing to end-use.

My only regret is that we did not have the confidence to jump in sooner. That is the first advice I would offer. Start with a small, achievable, project and go to a dummy mock-up as soon as possible. Ruthlessly copy others' design ideas and discover your own mix-and-match. Crucially we had gathered enough of a review panel and three start-up articles for submission which would show our range. We tried out colours – pleasant beige-yellow in a scrumpled background, and green bars – again getting away from the 'printy' look but also allowing maximum clarity. Dave (exercising his expertise as Disability Officer for the University) was concerned that pages should be clear and readable.

So we established some key founding technical and design principles:
1   the site architecture and how it structures its units or pages,
2   navigation,
3   colour, backgrounds and instant recognisability for this journal,
4   font and images, and
5   avoiding the 'printy' and so rethinking the logic of the 'page', banning 'volumes' or 'issues'.

There had to be an attractive overall design and easily navigable architecture. You could journey back-and-forth from each page via a clickable menu at the bottom so there were no 'orphan' pages. Backgrounds had to be pleasant – we avoided black-on-white – but allow maximum readability. Each of the articles has a different background and some small variation in design.

All files had to be simply named and in a one-word-plus-number combination (for example, 'garner991'). Remember that short compact file names help non-Mac users and those on pre-Windows PCs: the latter have difficulty with file names which are over-long or in which there are blank spaces between words. We had to be aware of those using older browsers and what would be their default presentation. It also helped that we could consult Jakob Nielsen's 'useit.com' web site at http://www.useit.com. There he dispenses swift and opinionated design wisdom to all, especially business users of the Net. He has regular 'Alertbox' columns and updates his 'Top Ten Mistakes in Web Design'.

Another early question was which software to use for site construction and maintenance. We tried out FrontPage but, although I am no computer novice, I found my apprenticeship on it too difficult. It does offer an attractive 'map' of links and site components but I decided I had to go for fast results. Since I do most of the designing and all of the data-input I settled for Adobe Page Mill and HTML. Sometimes I use the (lazy?) start-up in Microsoft Word, then save it into HTML. Glitches and fine-tuning are sorted out in Notepad. This is the speediest method that we discovered and fits in with our need for a streamlined production schedule.

Then we had the debate: frames or not? This decision was key to our planning of the whole navigation system. We decided against using frames, partly on Nielsen's principle of 'Frames: Just Say No'! Our site uses relatively simple architecture at present. Clicking from the main index page, users are offered:

> ARTICLES (Articles sub-home page leading to the sub-site of separate articles) + SUBMISSIONS + REVIEW PANEL + SDFVA HOME (hosting department) + UKC HOME (hosting university) + RADIO THEORY SITE + WFAE SITE (World Forum for Acoustic Ecology) + LINKS (radio, film, etc.)

The main home page however, for obvious marketing reasons, offers direct access to:

> SUBMISSIONS + REVIEW PANEL + ARTICLES

These pages would later grow into sub-sites of reviews and creative sound works. Users move through the cascading pages not via frames but by single navigation actions, and there are up to nine clickable options that are easily made available on every page (usually spread across the bottom, occasionally the top).

I can well see the advantage of frames on other sites though they discomfort some users in as much as URL links (including bookmarks) may stop working and frequently problems may be encountered with printing and using the back button. I have experimented with frames in constructing other web sites, however, and found most of the problems surmountable by following advice such as that obtainable on Jakob Nielsen's site http://www.useit.com. But for *Sound Journal* we designed a click-through site that requires only simple navigation by a straightforward choice of options and easy use of the back button.

Business sites frequently put the organisation's logo in the upper left corner of the screen which, when clicked, takes the user to the main home/index page. We chose not to use such a visual logo for *Sound Journal* but to rely on repeated choices at the bottom of each page to reinforce identity. The first option of these (bottom left) is invariably 'WELCOME PAGE' (I use the term 'WELCOME PAGE' instead of 'HOME' just for its cheeriness!) and other options offer global navigation options including ARTICLES (which then allows local navigation into this sub-site).

Then we worried over the *Sound Journal* home page, our front door. Again, looking at design alternatives on some other e-journals, we knew it had to fit totally within the screen frame. There must be no uncomfortable scrolling down because some visitors simply would not bother with that and it could vex other browsers. Also, as the top words would be picked up by search engines, they must give crucial information: '*Sound Journal* peer-reviewed electronic academic journal'. It is amazing how many academic and other sites do not respond to this need and allow, in effect, nonsense words to be picked up on AltaVista or other search engines. Those first seven or so words are an advertising slogan in cyberworld.

We experimented with placing an image (a .jpg) on this index page but then demoted it to a couple of other pages (SUBMISSIONS and REVIEW PANEL) because of the danger of an overly long download time. As Jakob Nielsen says in his 'Top Ten Mistakes', after ten seconds users lose interest. And bandwidth seems to be getting worse, not better, as the superhighway teems with more and more traffic.

For an alternative design solution to the index or home page, readers may care to visit *Political Theory*, the International Journal of Political Philosophy at Virginia Tech, USA (http://www.cddc.vt.edu/politicaltheory/index.html). This site is vivid and, in a manner of speaking, puts its goods at the front of the shop so that all the main information is found here: contents of the present issue along with the editorial board and seven images (Plato, Nietzsche etc.). The only downside (not a comment on the quality of this well-established journal, it is good to hail another independent!) is that this takes a time to download and then requires some scrolling down.

The brand image of *Sound Journal*, the logo, is simply the name in red against the yellow-scrumpled background and a green bar below. This red also stands out on those other pages which have different backgrounds. (Blue, as Nielsen points out, should never be used as it suggests a hypertext link to click on.) We wanted something that would suggest listening and audiences yet would endure as a brand image. We discussed what images we could use – a human ear (too medical!) – and decided that early technology was comfortingly retroist, universal and evergreen. We used a picture of a 1922 Marconi crystal set, on sale when the British Broadcasting Company first officially started broadcasting. This image also chimed with the seventy-five years celebrations of the BBC's foundation in 1998 (and some other celebrations to come). I own the copyright of this digital picture as I took it myself. This image was put on a couple of the pages – the details for submitting articles (SUBMISSIONS) and the peer-review panel (REVIEW PANEL). The font chosen for the site was Times Roman because it is a serif font and more accessible for users with disabilities. (But remember that text conversion can, wittingly or unwittingly, be changed by default at the user-end and that some users, for example those with dyslexia or poor sight, may prefer to convert your HTML font to a more comfortable font style/size.)

The ARTICLES page – which accesses the separate journal articles – is the most important business part of *Sound Journal*. As a sub-site it has a somewhat different colour and feel to it although it is consistent with the whole site. Here the most radical decision was necessary. We knew we would grow slowly and so we rejected from the beginning the concept of 'issues' and 'volumes': articles would not be organised into an electronic clone of print journals because, as Smith says, ' there is no real need for this unit on the Net. Old habits die hard!' (Smith 1999a). We felt that archiving could be organised later by means of a page giving an alphabetical listing by author and title.

Articles are presently listed chronologically, each with its date and accompanied by an abstract. The user has to scroll down and the presentation is a little more dramatic, being a background of out-of-focus print columns. Each item is separated by a narrow coloured band, fading on the left. The layout of the articles themselves includes these bands between the main sections and a double band at the close. (This coloured band is frequently used on personal home pages and recently by the British glossy 'TV and Satellite Week'. We wanted something popular but relatively discreet.)

After the title and author, the author's e-mail address is given (with permission) and the URL of the article. Unless this URL is placed in the body of the text and prominently at the top some users' printers can clip the standard URL printout and make this vital information unreadable. Another radical design decision – to provide a downloadable .txt version – is given as an alternative in order both to save on print costs and to make the site student-friendly. Each paragraph is numbered for ease of citation by scholars (one of the key objections voiced against electronic publishing). This also helps make an e-article more readable and quotable as well as making glancing and re-glancing at the text easier. This is part of our new 'logic of the electronic page' within the limits of the computer screen.

It still remains true however that, for many, print is the preferred means of reading material of any length (Harnad 1999). In my design, I have chosen to open out the layout and to use much more space, again making the contents more approachable for students. Even though Warkentin's survey of German studies in Canada notes that students were the smallest group of e-journal users (Warkentin 1997) my own experience suggests they are at least *significant* users. But am I alone in finding articles in PDF format (where the resolution is only 90 dots as against the equivalent 280 dots for high quality print) difficult to read on the screen? I admit these problems can be offset because PDF does allow the reader various options to alter the presentation on screen (and these options can be accessed through HELP on the Acrobat Reader programme) but that doesn't necessarily solve all the problems.

Fortunately linking footnotes back and forth has now become more common in e-journals than when we first started. Endnotes are linked to the appropriate number in the text with a BACK TO DISCUSSION + number link on each, for example BACK TO DISCUSSION (3.2). All this is for ease, clarity and the reader to be able to move back-and-forth comfortably. Endnotes and footnotes generally have this inbuilt difficulty of cross-referencing, though hypertext links obviously provide an easier solution than when reading print articles. However, it also has to be admitted that these guidelines demand considerably more labour on the part of the editor (Me! You!) in getting an article to screen.

And finally in this section, a minor tip about receiving text attachments from authors. Nowadays I always copy and paste such text first into Notepad and then into Word to remove any hidden formatting (especially that connected to such design features as endnotes). I learned this the hard way!

2. SOUND JOURNAL – FEEDBACK

Following the launch we were ready to receive users' feedback and to make better our mistakes. There were two main corrections. Firstly we cut down on the original name. Initially baptised *'Electronic Sound Journal'*, e-journals had become more plentiful and accepted so it was possible to shorten the title to *Sound Journal*. The second and biggest change was an editorial one: seeking to be more innovative we chose, with the consent of the authors, to display articles *before* peer-review in a 'pre-print' sub-site. In this we followed the model of the *British Medical Journal*
(see http://www.bmj.com/cgi/shtml/misc/peer/index.shtml).

Standard reviewing practice worked for the first two and very few changes were required by the peer review panel. However this system foundered on a controversial article, strongly argued (and well worth final publication in due course) which reviewers felt required considerable changes. As in any tough editorial situation, the editors had to carry on the negotiations as well as they could (and the article will be re-submitted shortly) but the review process delayed progress for far too long, adding to the same problem that is encountered in print journals. One solution has been to put submitted articles into an electronic area with a password so that everyone entitled to inspect them can do so speedily, and the last article accepted via this process was peer-reviewed and passed within four days.

So, at its best paperless electronic peer review has a swift turnaround. I circulate the draft article as an attachment and in the body of an e-mail (just in case the attachment proves problematic). Of course my reviewers, unpaid and conscientious, may respond at length and in different styles and behind the scenes I sometimes have to compose a short report from the sense of three or four commentaries. Such are the duties of an editor and inevitably some additional touching-up is required for the final layout.

We also discovered that making available authors' e-mail addresses – again, now customary – was beneficial. True it could prompt a flurry of messages from students at essay-writing time but it also served to extend the 'invisible college'. There were also other additions: we agreed on a mission statement for the home page and, following some e-mail discussion, we improved our copyright statement. This was felt to be particularly important as 'I'll be plagiarised' was frequently mentioned as one of the objections to e-publishing. That section now reads:

> 'Except as otherwise noted, copyright in all contributions remains with the authors. *Sound Journal* holds exclusive rights in respect of electronic publication and dissemination. The Journal may not be posted or in any way mirrored on the WWW or any other part of the Internet, or an Intranet, except at the official publication site.
> Subject to this, permission is granted to download articles for off-line reading, within the following conditions:
> 1 If printed and passed on, no charge is made for the copy.
> 2 The author's name and place of publication, and any copyright notice, remain attached to any copies.
> Permission to download articles for educational purposes is granted, subject to the following:
> 3 Downloaded articles may be stored electronically on disk, as long as no charge is made for access, and access is limited to a known group of users with the educational institution.'

In the case of small independent journals scholars retain control of their copyrights as a means of securing the greatest possible flexibility in publishing. Copyright is hotly debated and I recommend John Sutherland's useful article at http://www.lrb.co.uk/v21/n01/suth2101.htm and the Declaration on Academic Writers' Rights by the Authors' Licensing and Collecting Society.

3. *SOUND JOURNAL* INTO THE FUTURE

What of the future? The review panel urge me to advertise in other journals and to post fliers to departments and conferences. I will do that as soon as I can gain a budget, the 'costless' regime can only last so long! There are some cost-free methods, however, and I have worked at listing *Sound Journal* in search engines and wherever I can find university lists of electronic journals and bibliographies. Also, Dave and I regularly look at other e-journals to see the best of what others are doing and it is interesting to note, for example, how *Sociological Review* [Online] has progressively improved its readability. There is also the *Journal of Electronic Publishing* at http://www.press.umich.edu/jep/ for the larger issues of debate.

But be ready to face unforeseen difficulties. For example we have just had to suffer a change of URL as our host university changed its overall address. This required burdensome extensive data-changing and is embarrassing because one of the objections to e-publishing is that it is here-today-and-gone-tomorrow: reliability and consistency into the future are the essentials of an e-journal.

Also be prepared for negotiations (particularly copyright) to prove difficult. In our case negotiations with BBC World (the business section of the BBC) on sound clips from radio plays and features could mean financial costs of anything from £500 upwards – and that for a one-minute clip for one year only (as negotiations have to be conducted with each artist and through agents who can show a tendency to treat every possible transaction as a cash cow). At the time of writing (spring 2000), partly due to the launch of a variety of electronic services, the BBC does not have a coherent policy on rights management for digital resources. My impression, following meetings, is that even senior staff can be unaware of the legal position and niceties of, for example, quoting clips. Also be aware that any copyright holder is likely to be wary; for example the BBC could potentially be embarrassed by any links from other sites back to them. So it follows that the only sound clips we use or hope to use in the future are those which are costless and copyright-cleared.

No journal can stand by itself so we have sought links to other enterprises. To encourage research and possible contributors I founded, with Tim Crook of Goldsmiths College, London, an annual radio drama conference. Radio studies as a subject area has now finally formed a national organisation and I have set up a linked site, including bibliographies, called 'Radio Theory' (available at http://www.ukc.ac.uk/sais/RSN/index.html). Linkability is all for a journal. I have also set up a test site for *STP* both for archiving and to encourage supplementary e-publications (available at http://www.ukc.ac.uk/sais/stp/index.html). In my paper to the editorial board of *STP* I suggested the following advantages:

- as a multimedia e-publication it would respond to the diversity of performance and help exchange creative research and skills, encourage the internationalism of research and make *STP* more available to students

- A supplementary e-version of *STP* would allow links and lead to a wider range of research outcomes
- It would be 'hot' in disciplinary terms – where the time taken to publication must relate to the need for the latest data, production and styles
- As added-value, I have already begun archiving out-of-print issues beginning with *STP* Number 10 (December 1994).

One of the first true electronic journals was E.M. Jennings' *EJournal* of 1989 (Smith 1999a). Yet a decade and more later Steve Harnad still laments that 'the biggest brake on progress is the reluctance of authors to entrust their work to a new, unproven, medium in place of the ones that served them faithfully for years' (quoted in Smith 1999b). Running an independent e-journal gives scholars flexibility and control at a time when print journals face spiralling costs. In subject areas where there are limited numbers of developers I see the future in empowering technology to fit our values as scholars and teachers.

But my responsibility as an editor of a small 'independent' is continuously to assure my contributors and readers of quality, credibility and reliability. I predict there will be a revival of the scholarly monograph, published independently on the web (even though at present it has been mostly squeezed out of print budgets). I am grateful to Steve Harnad and John Smith, among others, for so effectively arguing the case for the independents in many free-to-view articles on the web, even though their personal interest is 'STM' [science, technical, medicine]. My – our – biggest task, in promoting the e-journal, is confidence-building in academic colleagues, a clarion call for more 'invisible colleges' of scholars to get e-publishing and doing it for themselves, not least in setting up their own departmental web pages for students and getting them interactively involved.

2.5: Digital Dialogues
by David Hughes

1. WHAT IS DIGITAL DIALOGUES?

Digital Dialogues is a computer-mediated, web-based multimedia collaborative educational environment delivering critical theory, contextual studies, art history, research methodology and image manipulation teaching materials.

It is not technology driven. It aims to use technology to support pedagogic aims and principles and is designed to facilitate, encourage, support and motivate student learning through engagement and interaction.

It combines key primary and secondary texts, annotated by tutors, transcripts of lectures and multimedia resources. Completing worksheets within each named seminar, the student is constantly prompted to answer questions which will reinforce their understanding of the texts and complete exercises that invite them to write their own explanatory, analytic and critical texts following and reinforcing sound academic principles.

The multimedia resources of sound, image and video provide immediate illustration and practical application for the theory. Being web linked, the research potential of the Internet is constantly at hand and currently the Microsoft Exchange family of applications (the learning environment that houses the Digital Dialogues web pages) allows students to engage in online seminars as a group, with the tutor and in private chat rooms as collaborative working clusters.

1.1. A brief history of the project

Digital Dialogues began life as a response to the need to deliver, to a large student cohort, courses in critical and contextual studies and digital image manipulation. With online teaching and learning resources, online seminar and student feedback mechanisms, a small number of staff would be able to monitor and provide support for all the cohorts engaged with the system. Our experience of using Information Technology with students in practical performance projects and text-based bulletin boards suggested that we could enhance the learning environment by the use of IT and digital media, thereby increasing student engagement and motivation.

In the academic year 1996–97 I was running a module I had called 'Postmodernism and Performance' and we were dealing with the book *Masters of Deception* (Quittner and Slatalla, 1995) about young computer hackers in America. We were using computers to hold online discussions and seminars and we developed and maintained a bulletin board where people invented identities and narratives. There was a heady mix of fact, fantasy and theory. It worked. It was motivating. Students were making terrific work on and through the system, sometimes manifest as site-specific events and live performances but heavily informed and energised by the computer community. It seemed too good to be true. We should use this kind of system with its promise of delivering text, image, sound, video and all kinds of teaching materials to deliver critical studies modules; we wanted to enter digital culture; we wanted to be able to continue the dialogue that was the basis of all work with our students. We'd called it Digital Dialogues. Everyone hated the title: we still do, but now we're stuck with it and worse, the whole faculty knows it as DD or even Diggidogs. Hint number one: naming a project is like naming a child. They have to live with it for the rest of their lives!

What was also alarming at this point to my colleagues was that most of them did not have a computer on their desks or even within reach. How could we attempt this complete re-engineering of an undergraduate course in contemporary arts without access to computers ourselves and, more, without the skills that come from access and familiarity? This was addressed by a strategy to access more and more and better and better computers through means fair and foul. Even now, four years down the road, some of my colleagues still have bits of plastic on their desks that look like the dummy computers they use to decorate beech veneer workstations at IKEA. Another thing we didn't think about at the beginning, but which became highly significant, was the speed and specification of the machines being used. There is very little point in waiting for minutes for one piece of software to load or to access one web page: if you can't get the right kit for the job then the good work you do in design or in preparing teaching materials might go completely unappreciated. It is important to get each link in the chain right: the material is delivered through a desktop machine which has to have the right software, the right speed, memory, video screen and so on; browsers need the right plug-ins for the kind of media viewers you want to use; the connection between that desktop machine and the server needs to be fast; the server needs to be able to deal with the demands made on it by the numbers of students using the system; the link to the Internet needs to be fast if you are building in a concept such as the 'library without walls' (which is to say your in-house electronic library and the Internet becoming seamlessly connected research resources).

On the other hand it has been necessary to get on with the job in good faith and indeed the University's Computing Services, seeing our level of use, has subsequently provided suites of new PCs with excellent specs. A short-term ironic downside of that, however, was the rare event that initially the new specification was *too* high! So problems can arise when you least expect them. In this instance, the server which had been identified for our use was now too old and slow for the new workstations, resulting in only a few students being able to log on at once: we had to move to another server with a bigger capacity 'pipe' linking it to the network. This is the kind of thing that really needs very careful pre-planning. Another problem of this kind that we encountered was designing on a Mac and then delivering on a PC: all kinds of things don't travel well from one platform to another (such as fonts) and you have to ensure that what you work hard to achieve on the design machine is what you are going to be able to deliver on the students' desktops.

Whilst my colleagues were alarmed at the prospect of having to come to terms with cyberhorror there was undoubtedly excitement about the work being done on the 'Postmods' module. The computer element allowed the students to be creative, to play, to improvise, to collaborate and also to think, to read, to discuss (online) and to return to discussions again and again after reflection and to revise and rewrite and question. We had high hopes for Diggidogs if it could bring the same experience to the study of critical and cultural theory.

We subsequently introduced VAXNOTES, the system we had first used on 'Postmods', as an online chat, seminar and tutorial system for third-year students as a supplement to live seminars. We found, perhaps predictably, that the students who spoke less in class were very articulate and prolific online, and that overall there was an altogether higher level of engagement with and analysis of theory because the students could take more time making their contributions and could return to issues after online sessions and develop or add to them.

Our project attracted a great deal of attention. Dr Hugh Miller, from our Faculty of Social Sciences, was researching 'net identity', precisely this creative aspect of invention in the process of writing online. He brought his enquiries to our work and developed ideas and strategies with the students. The Centre for Learning and Teaching became interested as they were in the process of developing teaching resources and new strategies for delivery as a result of which they offered us loads of really old equipment! But they did try to help! And at least they set us up to start scanning and working with more software with the students. They also helped us make a bid to a Staff Release Fund run by Staff Development which allowed me a day a week for a year with a group of three very active and aware graduates who worked with me on learning environment, networks, servers and the design of our web site. We had decided that DD would essentially be a web site which delivered the teaching and learning materials and we really explored the nature of play in cyberspace, linking that with evolving design concepts and to the notion that students really should be able to customise their own online learning environment. Two elements in the design which we felt worked well and appealed to students were using the London Underground map (Fig. 7) as the basis for the site design of our 'Structuralism and Semiotics' modules and to have little witty animated GIFs (such as one of Freud reading in his garden (Fig. 8) on the navigation page of our 'Psychoanalysis' section and a great image of Elvis on a ground of pink in the Popular Culture area!).

We spent months researching different methods of prompting the reader to *think*: exercises which would reinforce good academic practices such as summarising and structured essay writing but also rigorous analytic *thinking*. We identified many texts that would provide the 'reader' for the project and sketched out the whole of the critical studies modules from year one through to the third-year dissertation. At that time this of course was being delivered through the conventional lecture seminar formula but, as the whole staff team became more involved, this had the effect of enhancing the role of critical theory across the course and providing an underpinning. It's also to be hoped that our students did become better at thinking and using concepts as material in their art making.

So we continued with our experiments in DD because by then we believed that it was our responsibility to give our students a good 'digital education' in preparation for the world they would be leaving us to enter. Besides which, by this time, we were all nerds anyway and liked playing with computers!

1.2. The development process

Primary, secondary and tutor generated texts (such as lecture notes and annotations to primary texts) for modules such as Structuralism, Psychoanalysis, Feminism and Postmodernism were identified and edited to a size where they could be read and worked on in a two-hour work slot. We thought two hours was more than sufficient time to be trapped in front of a source of radiation. Due to copyright restrictions texts were not made available online but were printable

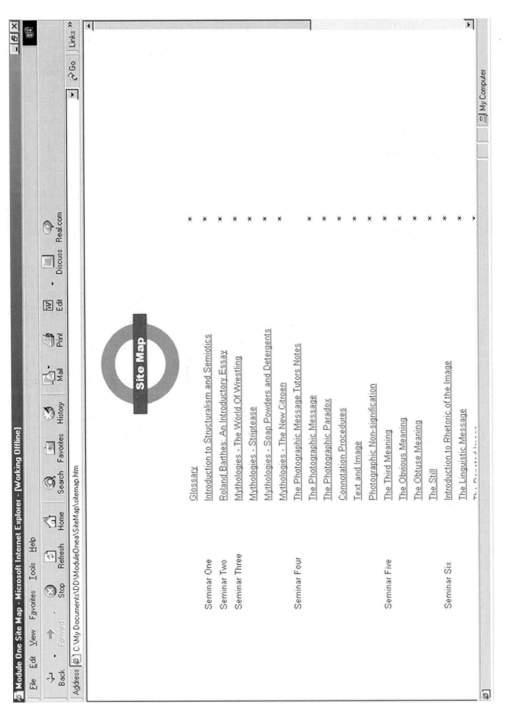

Figure 7: The environment of the web pages are enlivened by the use of images. The web site design is based around a facsimile of the London Underground

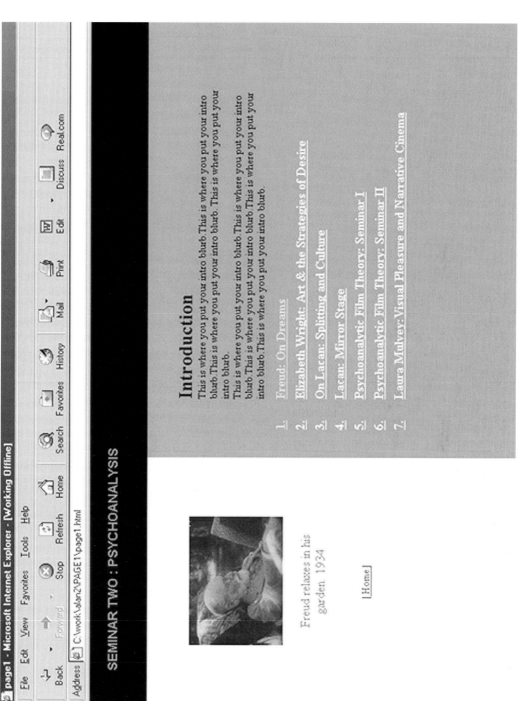

Figure 8: The image of Freud relaxing in his garden is the final still of a short film available on the web site

(with permission) as a private research copy so that only the responses to the texts were entered online. This also made it possible for students who preferred to work that way to read the texts in print form and to use *handwriting* to make notes! (Strange, I know, but some people still work that way.) Three strategies were used for prompting engagement with the texts: students were asked to:

a   make a judgement or provide an answer to a question on what they have just read for their own benefit or

b   to reinforce some point in the text, given a short reading guide or explanation or

c   asked to complete an exercise for return to the tutor for marking.

The following year, 1998–99, we were awarded a major grant from the university's Teaching and Learning Enhancement fund specifically to finish the development of the project and to implement it across the whole course. By now we had a notion that it could be used in almost every module and we were keen to create an architecture and a set of guidelines that everyone, staff and students alike, could use and develop in their own ways and for their own purposes. Currently we use the Digital Dialogues concept on our 'Critical Studies' modules, our third level 'Dissertation' module, our first level 'Approaches to Research and Writing' module and our second level 'Research Methodologies' module. Support for digital manipulation through Dreamweaver, Photoshop and Quark is also available online as is support for study, essay writing, use of English and research methodologies. The main practical teaching/learning methodology continues to be via worksheets that take the student through a series of moves in order to achieve a number of ends. This provides the basic skill set from which the student can extrapolate other actions and solutions.

At the point when we started to integrate critical studies into our course we realised that no convenient 'reader' existed (that is, no course-book or Computer-Aided Learning package that satisfied the course's need to teach a multi-disciplinary mix of critical theories, art histories, cultural studies and philosophies). Whatever we put together would have to provide all these texts and constitute a reader. If the computer-mediated teaching environment was to equate with the lecture/seminar format then we realised that a multimedia platform was essential to conduct illustrated lectures, seminars and tutorials which referred to visual, three-dimensional, electronic, filmic, sonic, digital and performative (time-based) works of art. The major outcome we expected from the teaching of theory was that students should be active or interrogative readers and so we perceived the need for an interactive learning platform that allowed reinforcement of learning, active rather than passive readership, dynamic understanding and assimilation, a collaborative educational environment and the potential for online, synchronous and asynchronous tutorials and seminars which allowed for student-staff, staff-student and student-student communications. This entire development was informed by our view that throughout their experience of the course students should acquire those key and transferable skills in information and digital technologies essential for employment and further academic study. Dialogue was essential, allowing the student group to discuss and work in collaborative groups within itself and with the staff. (Fig. 9)

7 Learning Outcomes

7.1 Knowledge and understanding in the context of the subject
- Research skills and methods to make and critique art.
- Comprehension of interdisciplinarity and hybridity in art practice in terms of both form and methodology through the process of making new art works.
- Historical and contemporary artistic and critical practices and discourses
- The social and political context of art and critical practices.

7.2 Cognitive skills
- Ability to formulate and test concepts.
- Ability to assimilate and synthesise diverse ideas.
- Ability to question assumptions
- Analyse and evaluate art works and texts
- Ability to bring appropriate critical concepts and discourses to bear on given situations.

7.3 Subject specific practical/professional skills
- Demonstrate the skills necessary to research, devise, produce and critique art works.
- Ability to identify a role and context for ones' practice and activities.
- Acquire and deploy appropriate technical, material and aesthetic skills within particular projects.

7.4 General/transferable skills (including key skills)
- Capacity to learn in and from familiar and unfamiliar conditions.í:
- Ability to initiate and manage own learning and work and to work independently.
- Ability to work with others either through negotiation, collaboration, in groups or teams.
- Ability to communicate (verbally, visually, textually, etc) effectively and appropriately and to select 'language' according to context.
- Competent use of IT e.g. word processing, communication, research.
- Confidence to approach and take on unfamiliar technologies processes contexts.

7.8 Qualities, skills and capabilities profile
Intellectual
- Critical reasoning
- Understanding/applying concepts
- Flexibility/adaptability
- Problem solving
- Analysis and interpretation
- Questioning assumptions
- Confidence to approach new and unfamiliar discourses and concepts

Practical
- Research skills and methods
- Practical skills in workshops, studios, sites, exhibition spaces
- Practical skills in relation to materials, space, time
- Professional skills related to identification of contexts and articulation of position
- Skills in the production of proposals and documentation
- IT skills such as word processing and web searching as part of research and the production of documentation / essays
- IT skills as required for practical projects – such as musical sequencing and web design.

Personal & social
- Understanding of audience and different cultural contexts
- Independence/self-reliance
- Self-motivation
- Planning and organisational skills
- Learning skills
- Enterprise and resourcefulness

Figure 9: Example of learning outcomes

2. THE COLLABORATIVE LEARNING ENVIRONMENT

In 1998–99, whilst trying to determine which collaborative learning environment would be most suitable to deliver the elements listed above, we had chosen FirstClass (a dedicated learning environment produced by Soft Arc). In ideal conditions it is customisable, accommodates all kinds of digitised and multimedia material, allows students to share their views and perceptions and to discuss them over a long period of time which allows reflection and change of opinion. Due to complications arising from accessing FirstClass on PC-based clients from a MAC server, there were problems with the presentation of web page files within the environment. It was not possible to place an icon for an html file (a web page) in a folder that could simply be clicked on to open the application and the file. However, by converting files to Acrobat Reader (.pdf) files, they could be lodged in the folder environment as icons and opened easily. There were advantages to using .pdf; in particular the desktop could be more easily arranged and scaled to accommodate work pads, Digital Dialogues' (.pdf) worksheet windows and online quick-response conferencing windows. The downside of using .pdf was that it was necessary to reformat the already-designed web pages completely and reinsert hyper-links.

So we also explored Microsoft Exchange but found, at that time, that it simply could not accommodate the range of materials we wished to use in a logical spatial format and did not allow customisability or real time chat. However, more recent developments are extremely positive and promising and it is now possible to put together a suite of resources (online chat, whiteboard, threaded discussion and so on) with shared folders and the scheduling, contacts and e-mail resources of the Exchange family and seminar- or module-specific folders containing teaching and learning materials and other multimedia resources. The front end of this suite can also be customised so that it can provide a branded 'front door' for access into the specific learning environment that is ideal for distance learning. This has the advantage over FirstClass of being fully integrated within our particular university e-mail and software support system and thus is much more familiar to our group of students. We are moving over entirely to this particular virtual classroom environment in the academic year 2000–2001 (Fig. 10).

3. ONLINE SEMINARS

Whilst worksheets had been prepared by identifying, editing and annotating key texts, the major research carried out in 1998–1999 was in online seminars. Here students sitting all over the university and potentially at home have a written seminar which they can all read on their screens as each new addition is made to it and can return to the transcript at any time. My general response to online seminars is that the first few times the students 'attend' them they are very playful and difficult to control. Space is non-hierarchical and you as the tutor cannot set up a visual dominant focus. If the students choose to ignore you it's difficult to make them acknowledge you!

When we did the first online seminar using Exchange (where the screen environment was simply an e-mail threaded discussion) the students had a great experience in terms of the novelty of the form of seminar but not much of my pedagogic agenda was achieved. Due to the time lag in replying and threading there was a very strung out, unfocused feeling to the exercise. This kind of system is fine if you are conducting discussion over a long period of time

The Nottingham Trent University
Virtual Learning
http://owa.ntu.ac.uk/learning

Home E-Mail Calendar Contacts Results Find Logout

Monday, April 3, 2000

News Board

Matthew please contact the Faculty Office!
Join in the discussion

Check the Surveying web site for new course information
Surveying Web

Contract Admin Hand-in deadline changed! new date is 5th April 4.00pm
Please fill in the Feedback Questionnaire!

WELCOME MATTHEW KELLY!

Course - BSC (HONS) QUANTITY SURVEYING-SW

Your Semester 1 Modules -

- DBE2011 BUILDING ENGINEERING SERVICES (SURVEYING)
- DCA2021 CONTRACT ADMINISTRATION: CONTROL
- DLW2101 LAW 2
- DSA2021 ADVANCED BUILDING TECHNOLOGY
- DSU1232 PRINCIPLES OF INVESTMENT MATHEMATICS AND STATISTIC

Your Semester 2 Modules -

- DCA3011 CONTRACT ADMINISTRATION
- DDA2011 DEVELOPMENT APPRAISAL & COST FORECASTING
- DSC2021 CONTRACT ADMINISTRATION: FINANCE 2
- DSM2021 MEASUREMENT OF BUILDINGS 3 (2)
- DSU1281 INTERDISCIPLINARY PROJECT

Useful Links NTU Web Site - Library Information Services - Student Union - Help Guide

Figure 10: Customised student desktop with access to Microsoft Outlook resources

– a semester, say – and you can read the new postings and respond to them during a particular period each day (in effect just like e-mail). But for online seminars a more immediate chat screen is necessary where all the writing appears in a long and immediately updated transcript on screen.

Rather than leaving the entire field open, and trying to bring some order to the dialogue, for the second Microsoft Exchange session I set up folders with specific questions forming their titles. This session proved to be much more focused and, I thought, academically more was achieved. But Exchange necessitates a number of moves to do anything and the whole thing was very slow with a time lag in delivery and retrieval. Also, because Exchange is the university's e-mail system, it was, we felt, in a way, too familiar and too public domain whereas FirstClass offered a more private, intimate architecture and can be personalised (which gives a sense of personal stake in the proceedings, of play and of the ability to design one's intellectual as well as interface environment).

The experience we had had in working with Exchange was replicated when we moved to FirstClass: a similar experience of wild play with subsequent focus. Whatever system is being used, the tutor needs to set up focusing strategies and methodological protocols or there is only play, not play in the service of engagement and motivation.

To develop and respond to these experiments further we also began working with Virtual World software from Active Worlds (where students can very literally design the spaces in which they learn as 'three dimensional' virtual worlds employing avatars to negotiate them).

However, it's important to note that due to our experiences with the complexity of administrating FirstClass and the inability to run it on our servers we eventually reverted to Exchange. We now invoke the familiarity of Exchange as an advantage once again!

4. STUDENT ENGAGEMENT AND MOTIVATION

The main problem with motivation has been computer illiteracy and phobia. We are addressing this by inducting all our students into the skills necessary to engage with Digital Dialogues through such first level modules as 'Approaches to Research and Writing'. However, we find that even thorough inductions, which are designed to demystify the hardware, software and technology, are not enough to cure techno-phobia. There is a real issue, we find, with a great number of our students who do not seem to have developed habits of concentration on anything – books, film, thinking. There is clearly the potential for immersion in computer games and this level of immersive activity is what we wish to replicate. However, this state is not necessarily the best state for the kind of distanced, critical thinking necessary to the analytic activity we are encouraging, so this question of engagement and motivation remains a live one.

'Approaches to Research and Writing' introduces students to electronic research methods, critical writing, essay writing skills and the basic critical vocabularies, tools and skills necessary to engage with all the critical practices embraced by the course. The module uses a thorough introduction to the critical methodology of structuralism as the pretext to deliver and reinforce those aims. Students are constantly prompted to recognise good argumentative practice in the structure of the key texts, they are asked to write short responses to questions which effectively provokes them into defining terms, looking up what they don't know or summarising key sections of a text.

The module now operates on the principle of worksheets that take the students through a series of tasks or actions that lead to the generation of an outcome. Thus the student has executed a series of moves that form a model for achieving similar ends across a range of applications and situations. They have explored the basic architecture and logic of the system and this should be transferable to other systems and situations.

The module runs through basic computing skills (e-mail and word processing), electronic library skills leading to a bibliographic exercise, summarising and comprehension exercises, critical writing exercises, essay writing exercises, workshops in Photoshop, Dreamweaver and Quark Xpress. The module effectively then introduces the student to the whole range of packages and resources that they will be expected to use during the course.

Research activities using the university's electronic library and the Internet are linked to the theory work that the students are doing in their 'Critical Studies' modules and they are invited to present research outcomes (essays, reports, surveys, etc.) in the form of web pages or Quark documents illustrated by images grabbed, created, manipulated or treated in Photoshop.

5. KEY AND TRANSFERABLE SKILLS

Information and digital technologies are now fundamental means by which we experience, understand, interact with and analyse the world and we wish to integrate these technologies into our teaching and learning systems to facilitate students' development as both learners and creators within these systems. Key to the project is the aim of enhancing student learning by engaging their interest in the world of new technologies and enabling them to gain a competitive advantage in the employment and academic markets.

Dialogue is the condition of teaching in A&D or studio-based disciplines. Whether we are dealing with 'theory' modules or 'practice' modules, the basic exchange between tutor/student and student/student is fundamental to the learning methodology. In our development of Digital Dialogues we have felt it important that we retain as much as possible the possibilities of dialogue for two reasons: it is an effective pedagogic strategy and it confers transferable skills in communication and collaboration.

6. EVALUATION

Despite our recent volte-face, student responses to FirstClass were very encouraging:

1   Student 1 used FirstClass to stage a flame war between two remote computers. He used the chat room facility that allows many users to have real time (written) 'chat'.
He wrote:
> Everything is there on the screen – a history – for response to anything at any time. This is not confusing as you can see everything at the interface. What is exciting is the possibility of having many conversations at once, public and private. Responses are to visual stimuli not just the meaning of the communications that gives room for further play/visual punning. The whole transcript can be saved and printed out or saved to disk. This can be edited or manipulated making it available as another kind of material to be worked with.

2   Student 2 followed the 'Postmodernism and Performance' module, making visual interactive web based artwork. He reflected for us on the experience of online seminars using both Exchange and FirstClass.

He wrote:

> I thought FirstClass was far better in terms of conferencing than Exchange. I particularly liked the fact that it is so easy to apply and download images with the use of a digital camera (can we get one?). FirstClass had a logical flow and was really user friendly although it did have a fault, if you didn't type anything for a while it threatened to kick you off (cheeky sod!!!) That is as picky as it gets, though. Overall I preferred it to Exchange.

3   Joshua Sofaer, lecturer in Contemporary Arts leading the 'Postmodernism and Performance' module. Joshua reflects on leading online seminars using both systems.

Joshua wrote:

> FirstClass as a 'site' generated its own agenda. We came to the seminar with little to talk about – but found that the software engaged subject matter (partly but not solely because it was novel). We found ourselves relating to each other differently than in a normal seminar context. This sounds obvious – but I mean it in a more profound way than simply through the mechanics. The traditional pedagogical structure (teacher/students) became sort of flattened out, which meant that content issued from students in a way that it normally doesn't.
>
> The space does not allow for long messages – so it was next to impossible for someone to hog the space. People spoke/wrote in more of an even balance (quantitatively). It made more sense to move rapidly from subject to subject. The mechanics forced concise thought. Students were more inventive (again partly but not solely because it was a new experience). They were conscious of the freedom that the restrictions of FirstClass gave them (ironic really).

7. PRELIMINARY CONCLUSIONS

Evaluation of the overall educational environment, delivery and effectiveness of Digital Dialogues is currently being conducted under six headings of which the following are some preliminary observations:

i) student engagement:

When the elements of play, improvisation, and immersion are present, the engagement and motivation level is high. When there are clear and easy systems for feedback, chat, interaction with staff and other students and unrestricted opportunities for writing into chat rooms, threaded discussions or lists, the engagement and motivation is high. However, the atmosphere of the computer room is not ideal for focused work or for concentration. There are problems for students in relation to reading anything, and reading from a computer screen is neither better nor worse than the page of a book when this habit and culture is not ingrained.

ii) coherence of content:

The content of the online seminars has been developed in relation to existing module specifications and learning outcomes. The range of seminars is comprehensive and the existing architecture of the web site can accommodate further modules.

iii) ease of communication with fellow students and tutor through online 'dialogues':

FirstClass seemed to offer us this but technical and administrative difficulties prevented this from happening. Microsoft Exchange developments suggest that this range of dialogue facilities is now available and this is in development. Our experiences in designing conferencing, chat and list 'dialogue' will be brought to bear on the new system.

iv) value and relevance of navigational systems:

The major advantage of the Exchange-based system is that navigation is lateral: from the index or home page the student can move in one click to any of the other resources such as calendar, e-mail, word processing, library information services and so on.

Once the student has access to the index page for the Digital Dialogues web site then the specific module is one click away; wherever the student is within the seminar structure, they are only two clicks away from anywhere else within that module. They can easily return to the index at any stage from where they can move immediately to another link.

v) facilitation of collaborative learning:

Exchange will facilitate this through 'chat' mechanisms. Trials in practical modules where groups use online chat and threaded lists as means of communication show that IT can provide another channel for communication but have not yet proved, perhaps because we have not tailored a module to test it out, that IT provides a better environment for collaborative working than the studio.

vi) inculcation of interdisciplinary approach to critical studies:

The interdisciplinary approach is written into the content of the modules and, as such, Digital Dialogues simply perpetuates that ethos.

7.1. Summary

1   Digital Dialogues offers inductions into the skills essential for engaging with the Contemporary Arts Degree Course through:
- online synchronous and asynchronous seminars and tutorials;
- online digitised lectures;
- primary and secondary texts annotated by tutors;
- audio-visual illustrations and examples;
- constant encouragement to engage, question, critique and analyse;
- customisable desktop, links to other sites, support for essay writing, research methodologies and study skills;
- exercises to reinforce learning.

It also gives students a space to play.

2   What have we learned from our experiences so far? That:
- ownership, play, investment and the acquisition of transferable skills are important motivating elements;
- focusing strategies and methodological protocols set by the tutor to achieve objectives are essential.

The big question we will continue to deal with is how to get the balance between those two – freedom and discipline – to allow both pleasure in the system and rigour in practice.

Section 3: Digital Resources in Performance Practice

3.1: IT and the audio-visual essay
by Steve Dixon

This section aims to offer some help and practical guidance in utilising the audio-visual capabilities of IT to produce materials and teaching aids; to document performing arts practice; and to present research and critical 'writing' in new ways. It is particularly aimed at those who have relatively limited IT skills but are interested in beginning to create materials – the same position I was in when I produced my first CD-ROM. It begins by discussing some general issues to be considered when commencing an IT project, and goes on to use my *Chameleons 2* CD-ROM project as a case study to examine some specific methods and techniques, such as the 'audio-visual essay'.

1. MAKING IT EASIER

Producing audio-visual IT material is not as difficult or daunting as at first it might seem, and is not out of the reach of *anyone*, whatever their level of computer skills. For example, although it is clearly helpful to understand what various software and authoring programmes can do, it is by no means essential to know everything about how they work and how to operate them. Where a technical collaborator with the requisite skills can be found (or hired), it is unnecessary to spend weeks (on graphics programmes such as Photoshop) or months (on authoring programmes such as Director) learning how to use all the tools or programming aspects involved.

    I often work with students who can use the project collaboration as an assessed element of their course, and this considerably reduces the time I would spend completing all the design and programming work myself. Working in collaboration with technicians has another distinct advantage, just as it has in theatrical production. A theatre director who also attempts to design and build the set, edit the sound master, and rig and plot the lights, may become too bogged down in technical detail and lose sight of the piece as a whole. In the same way, the technical aspects of computer programming can become all-consuming, leading to what has been termed 'analysis paralysis', whereby 'the means become the ends as you forgot what you wanted to get out of the computer and become wrapped up in the process of getting it out' (Shu 1992, 6).

    In my own IT work producing CD-ROMs and electronic web articles, I write the textual material, record and edit all video and audio material (as I already have those skills), assemble stills and video for each section, and make decisions about design concept and navigation. But I leave most of the detailed interface design and programming aspects to technicians and collaborators who have the appropriate skills and experience. There is thus a close analogy with the theatre production model: I act as scriptwriter/producer/director preparing the central content and once this is completed, others come in to deal with design and technical operation.

However, whilst in the theatre many aspects of design and stage management necessarily run in parallel with (and develop in relation to) the rehearsal process, in my experience it is advantageous to separate the two broad stages in producing IT materials or producing CD-ROMs. The fundamental advantage is time – and associated costs if you are hiring a designer/programmer. For my first CD-ROM, I completed all my work and knew exactly what I wanted so that when Fraser Durie came in as designer to construct the various icons, 'pages' and hypermedia links, we were able to complete work within four weeks. A specialist programmer was then employed for a further two weeks to complete 'lingo' programming, run tests to locate and eliminate any 'bugs', and produce the master disk.

For the second CD-ROM a different schedule and approach was undertaken following the arrival of a German multimedia student, Thomas Jachmann, for a six-month stay to study and complete a project in our department as part of the Socrates/Erasmus European student exchange programme. Here, the writing of material, editing of video and audio, and (perhaps most crucially) my decision-making took place during the same six-month period Thomas worked on the design and programming. This piece-by-piece approach resulted in much wasted time and effort, as concepts and ideas about navigation and screen elements were continually revised and changed. As we were both working on small sections of an unfinished piece, we also frequently became bogged down in detail, endlessly tinkering with tiny design elements, and unable to 'step back' and see the wider picture. Nonetheless, this more 'organic' approach did result in a sophisticated and well-designed CD (Fig. 11). But the process was not without considerable frustrations, particularly for Thomas who would have much preferred to have had a clear concept, and a completed script and navigation map at the start.

2. DECIDING ON A DISSEMINATION FORMAT

In commencing a project, deciding on the ideal form to output or disseminate the material is a prime consideration. For conference presentations or teaching materials, it may be adequate to run the material from a hard or floppy disk, for example when using presentation software programmes such as Microsoft PowerPoint. For wider dissemination, when the content is largely text or still-image based, creating World Wide Web pages remains the simplest and cheapest option, with the advantage of global accessibility. Web design software programmes such as Macromedia's DreamWeaver and Flash, and Adobe's GoLive (Cyberstudio) have become increasingly flexible and easy to use, and have now overcome the need to learn complex 'html' programming language. Once created, the web pages or web site can be also be 'burned' (copied) to CD-ROM, retaining all its hypertextual features (including 'hotlinks' to other web sites), to enable use of the material offline.

CD-ROMs currently have a speed advantage over web sites since pages load far quicker, but for text and still image projects it is questionable whether this advantage (saving only a few seconds per page or 'click') justifies the move into more costly CD-ROM production –

Figure 11: Chameleons 2 *main menu*

particularly as modem and Internet speeds continue to develop. However, the transference of video and, to a lesser extent, audio over the net is generally slower and more problematic, and depends on the speed of the computer and the Internet connection of the end-user. CD-ROM (and more recently DVD-ROM) formats therefore offer considerable advantages. Video playback is instant and relatively smooth on CD providing the user's computer has fairly basic memory (32Mb RAM) and processing power (Pentium PC or Power Mac). Conversely, on the same computer, one minute of video may take as long as ten minutes to download from a web page, depending on the modem connection and Internet traffic.

3. UTILISING VIDEO IN DIGITAL FORM

I have produced two theatre-based CD-ROMs that document and analyse productions by *The Chameleons Group*, a performance research company I direct at the University of Salford (Dixon 1995; 1999). Although the dissemination medium is in digital CD-ROM form, the majority of the original documentation was recorded on videotape. Although we used professional video cameras (Betacam) and editing systems (Avid Media Composer), any video technology format can be adequately used. Nowadays, an excellent option is to use mini digital video cameras which have FireWire, such as the Canon XL1 or Panasonic EZ35, which are light, easy to use, and relatively affordable. FireWire (a Macintosh term) is also called 'i.link' by manufacturers such as Panasonic, or IEEE1394 in much of Europe. It enables you to input the digital video data directly into the computer for editing. A number of excellent editing packages are now on the market to edit video digitally on domestic-specification computers, and for ease and user-friendliness I'd particularly recommend Digital Origin's EditDV for PC or Macintosh, or Apple's FinalCut Pro for Macintosh only in preference to the ever-popular Adobe Premiere. Video takes up a large volume of disk space, so a large computer hard drive is necessary for any ambitious video editing ventures – five minutes of video takes up around one gigabyte of disk space.

Once editing has been completed, 'movies' can be compressed and saved in different formats and at varying resolution qualities and sizes. For my CD-ROMs, we saved the video sequences as QuickTime movies sized at 120 × 180 pixels, and running at 12 frames per second. This is a fairly standard size and specification within the multimedia industry, allowing relatively smooth video playback without taking up large amounts of disk space. At this size and running rate one can fit around ninety minutes of video within the 650 megabyte capacity of a CD-ROM. However, its size is relatively small on the computer screen, and I would suggest increasing pixel/window size and resolution if storage space allows.

4. PRODUCING *CHAMELEONS 2* CD-ROM

The documentation and CD-ROM production stages we adopted for *Chameleons 2* were as follows:

1   All steps within the process of devising the theatre performance the CD examines (exercises, improvisations, rehearsals etc.) were documented on videotape using a single camera, which the four performers operated.

2   A two-camera recording was made of a public performance of the production, which was later edited to produce 'The Show' tape.

3   Following the production, I wrote the commentary sections of the CD, and each of the performers also wrote personal reflections and critical commentaries about the production: specific scenes they had devised, their character development, and various other pieces focused around themes I had specified would be sections on the CD. We all then recorded our commentaries as voice-overs in a professional sound studio.

4   I drew up a 'navigation map' to map out the hypermedia links to each of the sections (Fig. 12). Navigation maps are conceived in one of four structures: *linear*, where users progress sequentially through a prescribed route; *hierarchical*, where more and more optional routes appear and spread out like tree branches as the user progresses; *non-linear*, allowing the user to move freely around without any predetermined routes; and *composite*, allowing generally free navigation, but also incorporating some linear or hierarchical structures (see Vaughan 1994, 390). *Chameleons 2* uses a largely hierarchical structure.

5   The video and audio material was edited using an Avid Media Composer digital editing system, and individual files and scenes were compressed in QuickTime movie format.

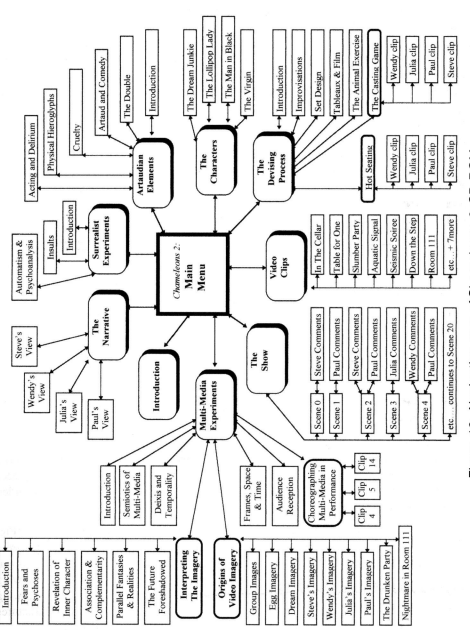

Figure 12: Navigation map of Chameleons 2 CD-ROM

'The Show' recording was edited and saved as 21 separate scenes, to speed computer loading time (it is generally advisable to keep digital movie files relatively short, ideally less than four minutes) and to enable users to select scenes and navigate around the one-hour performance footage easily.

6   Stills were captured from the video material of rehearsals and performance, and manipulated using Photoshop software to create graphical backgrounds, icons and interface environments for the CD.

7   Sequences bringing together the appropriate elements and files (pictures, movie and sound files etc.) for each of the sections were then constructed and programmed using Macromedia Director software, and hyperlinked in accordance with the navigation map. Director is an industry-standard authoring software, some aspects of which are relatively easy to use. Different format files (text, movies, images etc.) can be imported into 'cast lists' as 'sprites' and activated (made 'visible' or 'invisible') at different times. However, textual 'lingo' programming is also required to bring all the elements together, and it is advisable to get some support on this unless you have programming expertise, or are prepared to spend a considerable time learning 'lingo'.

8   A downloadable version of QuickTime software with installation prompts was added to the CD to enable users to install QuickTime on their computers in order to be able to play all the video and sound files.

9   Beta-testing amongst student volunteers was carried out to ensure the CD worked effectively.

10   In Director, all the CD material was converted into a 'projector' file, and a master disk was produced. It is worth noting here that Director gives you the option to save as a projector file for both (PC and Mac) platforms. However, it is generally considered that for a dual platform CD-ROM there are fewer complications authoring the material on a PC and playing it on a Mac than the other way round. I found this to my cost with the first CD in 1995, which was authored on Mac, and I finally had to release as Mac only – although more recently dual-platform conversion has been greatly simplified.

11   Design work for printing on the disk was produced, and the master CD was sent to a major CD manufacturer for duplication. Costs vary considerably here, but at the time of writing most companies have a set-up charge for mastering of up to £500, and CDs are between about 50p and £1, depending on quantity.

5. CONSTRUCTING AV-ESSAYS

The *Chameleons* CD-ROMs have two primary elements of content: performance documentation; and what I call 'audio-visual essays' – critical discourse presented in sound and pictures. These 'AV-essays' combine a voice-over commentary with changing visual imagery, screen environments and video clips that complement and (hopefully) illuminate the discourse presented. They aim to use the capabilities of digital multimedia to bring together theory (presented as a 'scholarly' voice-over) and practice (represented by images and video footage of live theatre).

The basic form of the 'audio-visual essays' constructed in the two *Chameleons* CD-ROMs derives from film and television documentary, where moving pictures combine with an audio commentary. A range of visual elements were used: video footage; animations; graphics; pieces of text; 'slide shows' of changing stills; stills building up on the screen as photomontages; and combinations of these. The still photographs we used were all taken from the video documentation footage. These were 'captured' using Photoshop software and a New Vista video capture card (now discontinued, but newer cards such as Miro are equally effective) and saved as 'JPEG' files. JPEG is now the most popular image format, largely because it is the standard picture file form used on the web, offering highly compressed but good resolution images. However, other image formats such as TIFF or PICT can also be used on CD-ROM.

For the first CD, the audio-visual essays were relatively simple, and primarily constructed using JPEG stills of varying sizes which were programmed to appear or change on screen at specific points synchronised to the voice-over. Some essays incorporated mute video clips, and for ease and to guarantee close correspondence between the voice-over and specific images or edits on the video, the audio commentary was edited alongside the pictures, as in a conventional TV documentary, and saved as a composite QuickTime movie file. The second CD made far more use of mute video during the AV-essays. However, as different sections on the CD used the same piece of video (sometimes with its 'sync' dialogue sound, sometimes mute), space was saved by keeping the voice-over QuickTime tracks separate, and 'calling up' video footage on screen whenever necessary from the central database of files. This avoided any duplication of the same piece of video.

For both CDs, each voice-over was recorded in a professional sound studio and then converted to QuickTime movie format (containing audio but no picture information) rather than a conventional audio file such as a '.wav'. We found we were able to synchronise and control the specific cue points ('in' and 'out') of the voice-overs that prompted stills to appear more easily and accurately using the numerical timeline information embedded within QuickTime movies, rather than using .wav or other audio-only file formats. Additionally, as the second CD was dual-platform (able to play on both PC and Macintosh) it was far simpler to use QuickTime, which both platforms recognise and play, rather than .wav files which are PC-specific.

6. CASE STUDY OF A SECTION: *THE DOUBLE*

The Double section of the *Chameleons 2* CD-ROM is a two-and-a-half minute AV-essay exploring our theatre company's practical applications of Antonin Artaud's theoretical metaphor of the Double, as articulated in his book *The Theatre and Its Double* (Artaud 1970). A large number of visual elements are used: 4 separate mute video clips; 3 photo-based animations; and 14 different JPEGs, some of which were themselves composite photomontages of several images, which had been created in Photoshop. In addition to the moving images of the QuickTime movie clips, there is thus visual 'movement' throughout the AV-essay as images and animations gradually appear and transform – on average at least once every ten seconds. Many of the images are 'cut-outs' of the stage characters. This is a technique we used throughout the CD to frame characters against a black background. It is extremely easy to achieve using either the 'magic wand' or 'lasso' tools in Photoshop which can be used to trace around figures or objects and cut them out from their original backgrounds.

The degree of frequency in visual screen metamorphosis made the sequence a complex and lengthy one to construct, and I do not suggest that it is entirely necessary to go to such lengths; if well conceived, far simpler or more minimal approaches can work equally successfully. However, it should come as no surprise that research testing in commercial multimedia applications indicates that a high frequency of change in visual screen composition is likely to increase user interest and engagement, as well as the frequency and the length of time (per sitting) that a user 'plays' the application. This has informed the development of a 'more is more' ideology of hypermedia, as propounded by writers such as Edward Barrett (1988; 1992), and George Landow (1992; 1994). In *Discourse Across Links*, David Kolb discusses how critical and theoretical writing is affected by the agency of new technologies. He concludes:

> In an inversion of Mies van de Rohe's famous dictum ... more is more: Let us have more links, more bandwidth, more images, more content ... Computers, and hypertext in particular, are often thought of as tools for the storage and manipulation of data. We have to come to understand the ways in which hypertext and CMC [computer mediated communication] move us beyond data access into the realm of discursive gestures and poetics. (Kolb 1996, 25).

The Double section transcribed below provides an illustration of how the principles of the AV-essay are applied in practice: the left-hand column is the audio voice-over; the right-hand column describes the visual elements that work in tandem with it. The screen imagery constantly changes and keeps pace with the theoretical commentary – a cumulative bombardment of image and discourse.

Voice-Over Commentary	**Visual Elements**
The interrelationship between the two modes of the live and recorded performance is central to our Group's artistic philosophy, and links to Artaud's concept of the double. Whilst this notion of the double is complex and multifaceted, in simple terms, our mise-en-scene enables the live performer to act out a character and narrative on stage whilst inhabiting a wholly different persona on screen. The screen dialectizes the subject, allowing simultaneous expression of the external and the internal, the social and the primitive, the conscious and the unconscious, the body and its double.	Photomontage of Julia pinned to the ground and a portrait of Paul. Video of the theatre scene the images relate to runs throughout.
	A Photographic Animation of Paul running is added.
	A second portrait still of Paul is added to the established photomontage.
	A third portrait still of Paul is added.
	A fourth portrait still of Paul is added to complete the photomontage (Fig. 13).
The concept of the body and the concept of space are both central to Artaudian theory.	The screen clears, a new photomontage

THE DOUBLE

Figure 13: A series of portraits are combined to create the first photomontage for The Double

Through the integration of a video screen within the theatre space we are able to experiment with techniques and effects which at times fragment and dislocate body and space, and at others unify physical and spatial significations.

Whilst video-based multimedia theatre has of course been around for a long time, the Chameleons Group are unusual in that the video texts are consistently performative, placing the performer as the central focus on both the stage and screen activity. The performers' bodies are thus located within two different spatial frames.

Les Essif has suggested that Artaud estab-

appears made up of a shot of Julia and a shot of Steve. Between them, a row of condoms, each containing an egg, hanging on a burning washing line (the flames are animated). Video of the scene the images relate to runs throughout (Fig. 14).

Screen clears. New photomontage of Paul and Wendy. Video of the scene the images relate to runs throughout.

A new still of Paul and Wendy is added to the photomontage.

Video continues, the rest of the screen clears, and a new photomontage appears: Julia and

Figure 14: Continuing photomontage from The Double

lishes a parallel between the emptiness of theatrical space and that of the psyche. He cites Monique Borie's assertion that 'the space of the theatre is space of creation, but is also the space of the perpetual return to the void' (cited in Essif 1994, 71). Essif believes Artaud transcends the Cartesian image of mind surrounded by void, by anchoring theatrical space to a central focal point, the vacuous mind at the centre of that void.

This dualistic concept of the void would link the metatheatrical to the metaphysical by ultimately referring to an internal world, a psychic space, like the metaphysical Balinese central dancer so prominent in Artaud's

Steve getting out of the car (mirrored on the video).

Photomontage changes to Steve falling on the car bonnet, having been shot (mirrors video).

Photomontage changes to Steve dead on the ground, the car in the background.

Photomontage changes to Steve and Julia both lying dead on the ground. The car has disappeared.

Screen changes. New photomontage of a cliff face with Julia and Steve's faces

Figure 15: Final image from The Double

theory' (*ibid.*, 71). The addition of an extra spatial frame in the mise-en-scene through a video screen creates another parallel spatial and psychic dimension.

But rather than using the recorded media to comment upon and objectify the stage action in a Brechtian sense as companies such as the Wooster Group or Forced Entertainment do, our aim is to create alternative perspectives and parallel fantasies to the stage action - trying to tease out the elusive 'double'.

superimposed, lit by candlelight. Video of new scene runs throughout.

Photomontage of faces fade out, cliff image remains. New, slowly animated photomontage of Steve preventing Wendy jumping from the edge of the cliff (mirrors video).

Animated photomontage is replaced by a new montage: Steve and Wendy embracing, then kissing (Fig. 15).

7. A NEW CRITICAL PALETTE

The convergence of information, sound, video and image presents a richer critical palette than monochrome words on a screen or the page of a book. The multimedia palette is also inherently suited to theatrical and dramatic presentation and interaction, as a number of writers have discussed (Laurel 1990; 1991; Norman and Draper 1986; Norman 1991; Heckell 1982). Digital hypermedia offers a radical new critical form and dissemination medium for contemporary theatre scholarship. The computer's ability to fuse together the written word with audio-visual representations of theatrical performances marks a significant advancement in the modality of performance research. In particular, the incorporation of searchable and programmable digital video footage of theatre performance enables the academic to construct a fluid audio-visual discourse which links theory to practice in a direct and tangible way. Computer technologies offer new metaphors, paradigms and codes towards a new visualisation of critical theory whereby the written critique and analysis is inextricably linked and fused with still and moving image representations of the theatrical artform.

> It is essential to realise that a computer is not a mere 'number cruncher', or supercalculating arithmetic machine... Computers do not crunch numbers; they manipulate symbols... Digital computers originally developed with mathematical problems in mind, are in fact general purpose symbol manipulating machines (Boden 1981, 16–17).

Academics and performance practitioners are both equally involved in manipulating symbols, be they theatrical or linguistic. New multimedia technologies offer a synthesis of written words and moving images, fusing together these traditionally polarised forms. Hypermedia programming offers unique and revolutionary possibilities for documenting, analysing and presenting performance research.

3.2: Shifting Grounds
Internet-based live performance work
By Sophia Lycouris

1. INTRODUCTION

Live transmission of sound and image through the Internet is increasingly used in contemporary arts not only as a means of distribution but often as an integral part of works which incorporate performance and/or live presence elements. Offering a number of exciting possibilities, this new practice also poses questions and brings new problems. On the one hand, practitioners constantly face a variety of technical problems which originate not so much in the lack of technical resources as in the vagueness of how and where appropriate technical support could be sought. At the same time, the ways, conditions, interfaces, manifestations of this type of work poses aesthetic and philosophical questions about the nature, the parameters and the meaning of such work. It is interesting to notice that the above two areas are closely related, intimately dependent on each other, intertwined in an unprecedented fashion. As technology (which has become the art medium in this case) develops and expands, the medium keeps changing; definitions, expectations and materialisations of ideas are constantly shifting. On the other hand, as practitioners work with whatever is technically available at any point, new needs are unavoidably identified, further technical solutions are sought and subsequently discovered keeping the medium in constant flux.

In their account of the 'technological' Michael Menser and Stanley Aronowitz suggest that the 'technological' should be explored from three methodological points of view:

> The first is *ontological*: what technology is… technology, science and culture all mix together along a continuum such that each object, to varying degrees, is the result of each of these three. The second is *pragmatic*: what technologies do; and the third is *phenomenological*: how technologies affect our experience in ways that are not bound to questions of function. (Aronowitz 1996, 15)

Rutsky, who believes that it is the changes in the very conception of technology (rather than the changes in technology *per se*) that really affect and interact with the domain of culture, does not seem to acknowledge this peculiar interdependence between technological shifts and aesthetic problems (Rutsky 1999, 1). However, he does accept that in the current postmodern moment (as opposed to the modernist area):

> the aesthetic can no longer be figured in the traditional terms of aura and wholeness, nor in the modernist terms of instrumentality and functionality. Like technology, it too comes

to be seen as an unsettling, generative process, which continually breaks elements free of their previous context and recombines them in different ways. (Rutsky 1999, 8)

In her discussion of the postmodern condition, Linda Hutcheon has suggested that the relationship between art practice and theory cannot be understood as a causal one but as 'a complex (interaction) of shared responses to common provocations', one that manifests 'overlappings of concern' (Hutcheon 1988, 14). Similarly to Hutcheon, who recognises the complexity of the relationship between practice and theory in the postmodern landscape, Rutsky is equally aware of the similarity of concerns between the aesthetic and the technological in postmodernism. Following a slightly different route, he seems ultimately to meet Menser and Aronowitz who, in their theoretical exploration of the connections amongst science, technology and culture have introduced the perspective of *complexity/complication*. Their theoretical position is fully equipped to accommodate the current fuzziness in the definitions of science, technology and culture as well as that of their in-between relationships. Moreover, as Menser and Aronowitz suggest, the use of such terms as *technoculture* or *technoscience* becomes a reminder of the indeterminate and hazy relationship between the technological and the human. In this context, it can be described as a metaphor for the indeterminate and *complicated* interconnection between live presence and digital technology in contemporary arts.

It becomes evident that the key parameters for such kind of work are really dependent upon the character of the constantly evolving relationship between the aesthetic and the technological. For this reason the quality of such work is never a matter of the degree of sophistication of the use of the technology involved, rather of how deeply aware of this relationship the contributing artists are. It is easy to understand, therefore, that it is possible to work with what might be considered 'basic resources' in this area and produce work of high quality if there is sufficient awareness of the medium (or type of technology) involved and its complex relationship with aesthetic decisions.

To give some indication about what is implied with the expression 'basic resources', the following six elements are necessary as a minimum for the works described below:
- a live performance space
- a web site (electronic space)
- a webcaster (an Internet provider that can support live sound and movement transmission)
- a telephone line
- a computer (minimum specifications of hardware: Pentium II, 64Mb RAM, 4Gb HDD, sound and video card, modem 56K but preferably ISDN, software: Real Player and Real Producer or Windows Media Player or equivalent)
- a videocamera

The videocamera, connected to the computer, records live sound and movement. Through the use of Real Producer, this digital information travels via an open phone line to the Real Server of the webcaster. The Real Server makes this recording available on a web site in the form of a Real Player files which can be watched by Internet users whose computers have Real Player. This basic process called webcast is of course used in a number of ways which have no relationship with artistic work. Yet that very process can easily become a method or even a medium to be manipulated, elaborated, expanded and challenged as part of an artistic process.

Drawing on the theoretical positions mentioned above, discussing examples of existing performance work which integrate elements of live transmission through the Internet, and addressing the technical idiosyncrasies of such work, this section aims at introducing the intimate interactive relationship between the artwork and its technology. The discussion concentrates on examples of work in the area of dance and technology. The questions explore conditions which allow for a reconsidered understanding of choreography, one which can accommodate the mutations taking place in work based on real-time processes, where digital technology has become a crucial component. Time, space and dynamics are key parameters in choreographic practice and extremely useful in this discussion; they provide a technical vocabulary through which methods in such practice can be looked at and elaborated upon. Notions such as architecture, representation and metaphor are also directly relevant to this discussion. They offer a hybrid vocabulary to address the *complexity* of the interdependence between the technological and the aesthetic.

Having emphasised the ontological, pragmatic and phenomenological aspects of the technological, Menser and Aronowitz's paradigm informs the process of constructing a methodology which can allow for a close investigation of the parameters of the above mentioned *complexity*. In Menser and Aronowitz's discussion, the ontological perspective introduces the question 'what is technology', the pragmatic point of view looks at 'what technologies do' and the phenomenological angle explores 'how technologies affect our experience in ways that are not bound to questions of function'. In the context of the investigation undertaken in this section, this paradigm reveals the importance of breaking the process down into three smaller tasks where a modified version of Menser and Aronowitz's methodology could be instrumental. The *complicated* relationship between the technological and the aesthetic in work which integrates live transmission through the Internet and movement-related elements and/or processes can be explored from three perspectives which are presented in detail below.

2. WHAT IS THE WORK?

Undoubtedly this is a question about the ontology of such work yet it involves a series of pragmatic elements. To discuss the nature of such work, one has to have access to clear descriptions. Such work incorporates new components in new ways, old components in new ways, mixtures of old and new components brought together in mixtures of old and new ways and so on. To be able to provide clear and accurate descriptions of what this work is, what its elements are and how they work together often becomes a fairly *complicated* process.

Here are three examples of descriptions of movement-based live performance work in which elements of webcast have been incorporated as these appear in the web sites hosting these pieces:

2.1. trans/forms (http://www.ad406.dial.pipex.com)

trans/forms is an ongoing multimedia collaborative project exploring the fusion of live performance with digital technology and online communication from an improvisational perspective. It includes a live improvised event performed by musician Viv Dogan Corringham and dancer Sophia Lycouris. Multimedia artist Nate Pagel interacts with the two performers using video projection and sound, which is a mixture of pre-recorded and digitally manipulated material of similar improvisations with live recordings from the event itself in combination with online contributions from remote participants. The projection operates as lighting for the event and the sound becomes an active component of its soundscape in constant dialogue with the live sonic contributions of the two performers.

The development of the project involves several stages of collaborative work and explores:

- the use of improvisation as performance mode emphasising the constructive dialogue between live performance and technology
- the character of collaboration primarily conducted through electronic channels of communication
- the aesthetics of multimedia artwork which combines live performance with digital technology and remote contributions
- the practicalities of using technology improvisationally and how this affects the decision-making process of the performers in live improvised work
- the potential of constructing a coherent conceptual framework which justifies compositionally the contribution of such technology in live improvised work by directly serving its artistic aims.

trans/forms was originally performed as part of International Dance and Technology 99 (Arizona) on 26 February 1999. The material for this performance was produced in three different places of the world: Tempe, Arizona, USA (movement, sound and video contributions), London, UK (sound) and Turku, Finland (video). It was mixed live on the web. The remote participants were:

- London-based musicians playing live from the studios of London Musicians' Collective in London, including saxophonist Lol Coxhill, Michael Kosmides who played theremins and Knut Aufermann who used a glove and live electronics, all of these attached to his body in order to produce a 'sound' dance.
- Finnish art students from Turku Conservatory and Turku Polytechnic who created a dance video piece for Finnish winter landscape under the direction of choreographer Satu Tuittila and co-ordination by Kai Lehikoinen, Head of Performing Arts, Turku Polytechnic, Faculty of Performing Arts.

2.2. string (http://www.ad406.dial.pipex.com)

string is an installation/live performance piece which addresses limitations in the use of the physical body and digital/Internet-based technology as part of live performance contexts. Through manipulating the threshold between two and three dimensional considerations of the physical space, the piece explores connections between the physical and the virtual. It proposes a hybrid multi-spatial environment which unfolds within a time frame strictly defined by the travelling of digital information between two different physical locations of the performance. *string*, which has been created by Michael Kosmides and Sophia Lycouris, was originally performed in London in January 2000.

2.2.1. How the piece works

components

- a movement-based solo in one location (location A), movement material is about and around physical limitations of the live performing body

- a computer connected to the Internet, a sound system, two video projectors (with a mixing desk) and 'live' video mixer/editor share the same space with the movement solo (location A)
- a sound-based solo (instruments: three theremins) in another location (location B), sound material created around the physical limitations of playing three theremins
- a video camera connected to a computer which is also connected to the Internet and a 'live' video camera operator share the same space with the theremin player (location B).

relationships of components
- the activity in the theremin player's performance location (location B) is recorded live on video by the camera operator (who creates the visual material following a choreographic score). This recording is then webcast live via the computer with the support of a webcaster
- the live webcast accessed through a web site is received by the video editor in location A and directed through a mixing desk to the sound system and video projector of this location
- the movement solo in location A is then accompanied by the sound of the theremins as (and when) received through the webcast (taking account of delays and possible interruptions of the transmission)
- the movement solo in location A interacts with the multiple video projections of the webcast (taking account of delays and possible interruptions of the transmission). The images are projected on various surfaces including the walls of that space and/or the body of the performer. The editing/mixing and spatial position of the images follows a choreographic score.

2.3. Sojourn at Alexandria (http://www.lissfaindance.org)

On June 17–19, 1999 Liss Fain Dance presented *Sojourn at Alexandria* in collaboration with Ed Payne at QuickDog Inc. and Peter Chang at Geographica. Sojourn is an exploration of the performance venue that expands the boundaries of time and space. Dancers onstage are joined by projected 3D images of dancers at a second location – projected around the world in an Internet Webcast. The webcast was produced by QuickDog and MRD New Media Entertainment. *Sojourn at Alexandria* has been choreographed and directed by American choreographer Liss Fain.

2.3.1. Project goals
- Probe the capabilities of technology and its application to dance performance and other art forms
- Create alliances between artists to generate new work through the integration of media
- Bring performance to a wider and different audience than ordinarily would see dance through Internet broadcast of live and recorded performances
- Provide an interactive experience for museum-goers, enabling them to view, combine or change elements of the performance as they wish.

2.3.2. Phase I
In June 1999, Liss Fain Dance, in association with Theater Artaud, presented *Sojourn at Alexandria* at Theater Artaud in San Francisco. The piece was inspired by the Great Library of

Alexandria. At the height of the intellectual and artistic sophistication of the Greeks in Alexandria, Egypt, during the 2nd and 3rd centuries BC, they built an extensive system of libraries; the dynamic intellectual environment represented by these libraries, and the visually dramatic setting of the city were the impetus for the dance. The artistic goal was to create a dance piece of heightened energy and intensity that grew from tightly structured and well-formed movement.

The goal of using the Internet was:

1   To simulate how a collaboration would occur in real time, over distance using the Internet (video, sound, still, etc.)
2   To broadcast the performance over the web in order to reach a broader audience.

2.3.3. Phase II

This phase has two objectives:

1   To test the Internet as a vehicle for sending images,
2   To design a performance that combines, via the Internet in real time, a dance performance and an event occurring at a second location.

The project collaborators are revising *Sojourn at Alexandria* so that the Internet is used to transmit pre-taped images of dancers shot at a second location. Once the Internet has been tested in this format, Liss Fain Dance will premiere a piece whose set is designed to incorporate images transmitted in real-time from a second site. The set designer, Mathew Antaky, is working with Liss Fain to create a dynamic staging that energetically and elegantly integrates the two elements.

2.3.4. Phase III

Phase III adds simultaneous live performance at two physically distant locations. We will use Internet technology to bi-directionally live-cast performances/events at two distinct locations within the Bay Area, with projections, monitors and speakers in each location to inform each group of performers of what is occurring in the other space. The occurrences at each venue will be integrated into those at the other venue.

3. WHAT THE WORK DOES

This pragmatic statement has also some ontological aspects as the problem of what such work 'does' is closely connected to how it has been put together, the nature of its constituent elements and the conditions under which some kind of architecture has emerged. At this juncture it is useful to introduce into this explanation the 'choreographic' elements of time, space and dynamics. For a new piece of work in this area to have some connection with the practice of choreography, the work must have evidence of use of these elements. However, because the conditions of making and performing such works are both new and different, the potential for shifting/expanding the already acceptable meanings of such terms is vast. This is the point where the interaction between technical conditions and aesthetic decisions becomes most crucial. The flexibility to move across the whole spectrum of possibilities between literal and metaphorical interpretations of such terms is essentially what makes such work possible or even conceivable. On the other hand, the ways in which technical solutions are approached and developed has to be based on quite sophisticated understandings of the notion of choreography and the role of time, space and dynamics in this practice, so that the clarity of the aims and methods can remain intact. In this process there is of course an extreme but, at the same time, quite possible option: that the work finally reaches a situation where its choreographic character has been negated, subverted, deconstructed, mutated. This is one of the most exciting possibilities, yet it really depends on an even deeper knowledge of traditional methods of choreography so that the makers have the tools to deconstruct those processes and at the same time keep clear the artistic aims of the work.

In Liss Fain's work *Sojourn at Alexandria*, the projection of live webcast clearly subverts traditional assumptions about set design in dance performances:

> With the advent of digital media, live dance performance has the opportunity to expand its boundaries in untried and powerful ways. The unique ability of the Internet to enable real time collaboration between artists – irrespective of distance – and between artists and audiences – irrespective of location – makes it possible to create performances that link artists working simultaneously in different locations. The potential of the Internet to expand the dynamic environment of live performance through the introduction of more complex visuals creates the possibility of new types of artistic alliances…
>
> Liss Fain Dance will premiere a piece whose set is designed to incorporate images transmitted in real-time from a second site. The set designer, Mathew Antaky, is working with Liss Fain to create a dynamic staging that energetically and elegantly integrates the two elements. (http://www.lissfaindance.org)

In *trans/forms*, the live improvisations recycle sound and movement material from *Stories in D*, a pre-existing improvisational live performance piece, which is processed at a number of different levels and through a variety of both technology-based methods and live performance practices. *trans/forms* becomes a reconstruction of *Stories in D* via the body memory of the two performers who re-visit movement and sound fragments originally devised for *Stories in D*. Yet this now happens within a new performance environment, structured and constructed through projections and recordings of these fragments, reshaped to their final form through a number of digital and analogue manipulations.

In *trans/forms*, the two improvising performers operate in an interactive space where video images of their own movements and recordings of their own sounds become improvising partners directed by the work of the multimedia artist. At the same time, as remote sounds and images gradually reach the terminal situated in the performance space and become part of the piece, their role is to disrupt the otherwise introspective journey of the piece. As the performance progresses through time, the piece is constantly fed by recorded versions of itself, internally accumulating fragments of its own fragments as it follows a close circuit pathway in a self-reflexive landscape. Yet, at the same time, the remote contributions create regular fields of interference and tension which destabilise the consistency of this inward spiral. The improvisational framework of the work fully justifies the compositional role of such juxtapositions which are the product of the specific ways in which technology operates in the piece and ultimately engender a double-coded meaning.

Improvisation in live performance is a compositional event defined by clear decisions which take place in the 'present moment', become part of the performance process and are, for this reason, irrevocable (Lycouris 1996). There are a number of parameters which inform the decision-making process, amongst which one of the most crucial is the performers' assumptions and experiences in relation to models of composition. Philosopher Gilbert Ryle suggests that 'the vast majority of things that happen in the universe are in high or low degree unprecedented, unpredictable, and never to be repeated' (Ryle 1979, 125) and 'thinking' itself, which is 'the engaging of partly trained wits in a partly fresh situation' (Ryle 1979, 129), involves the practice of improvisation. Whereas in traditional live performance contexts the process takes place through the application of the assumed models of composition which follows Ryle's rule within the limits of rather familiar grounds, in hybrid improvised work, which incorporates the use of technology, the heterogeneity of the participating elements intensifies the role of the unknown.

4. HOW TECHNOLOGY AFFECTS EXPERIENCE

To apply the phenomenological perspective suggested by Aronowitz and Menser on the analysis of movement-based live performance which incorporates live webcast elements, one really needs to elaborate further on *space*, one of the three key choreographic elements mentioned earlier in this section which seems to be the most crucial in this discussion. Moreover, one has to concentrate even more intensively on the interplay between literal (technical) and metaphorical uses of this term and the full range of possibilities between the two ends of the spectrum.

In *string* one of the main objectives is to experiment with a movement-based live piece which unfolds within a sonic environment constructed by remote and mediated sound materials. These sounds not only travel (through telephone cables) in order to reach the location of the movement performance but, when they arrive there, they also offer the possibility of their own visual integration in this environment through their video images. The video projections are used to manipulate the structure of the performance space by constantly changing the relationships between two and three dimensional space: integrating the shape of the body into the two dimensions of large projections (suggesting/ referring/representing three dimensional spaces) and/or mapping such images of small size on the sculptural (three dimensional) surfaces of the performer's body. Using superimposed textures on three dimensional elements (such as the performer's body) and integrating shapes of three dimensional elements into two dimensional projections are both strategies of negotiating the materiality of body and light.

In *trans/forms*, although the piece was conceived in such a way that the three artists (two performers and multimedia artist) have complete control of the process, the remote participants have the opportunity to provide means which could seriously disrupt the intimate atmosphere of the piece. The original improvisational material which was devised for *Stories in D* was based on sound and movement manipulations of fragments from everyday conversations. In *Stories in D*, the aim was to use movement and sound elements in order to magnify the intimate character of 'everyday life' moments as these appear in casual dialogues which are often ways of 'thinking aloud' in front of a witness. There was an effort to 'dress' these moments with distinct Mediterranean and South European textures, which would emphasise the play/contrast between interior spaces and outdoor locations and make the images and sensations stronger and clearer. This was primarily achieved through the use of an improvisational lighting 'score'.

In *trans/forms*, the movement and sound material are both re-visited, yet the lighting 'score' has been replaced by the use of projection, which is a radically different lighting source.

Lacking the 'traditional' lighting support, the location of the piece has been decontextualised. The improvisations have been suspended, trapped in some sort of indefinable time and space. In such an almost 'clinical' environment, they have become manifestations of 'pure' movement and sound forms. Yet, through the use of technology, parts of them have been magnified, emphasised, highlighted, but also modified. Projections and recordings bring the viewers closer to these imaginative intimate spheres, revealing to them some of their most unusual, distorted or ambiguous aspects. As the piece unfolds through time, it travels deeper and deeper within itself and makes its own fragments ever more available to the audience.

At the same time, because of the webcasting, the event has been opened up to 'the world'. The performance is virtually accessible to anyone globally who has a terminal and the appropriate connections, a large international audience who receives 'close up' versions of these intimate events, while having, through the option of remote participation, the opportunity to contribute elements to the process which could irrevocably alter the flow of the event. Notions of the private and the public become elements of each other in the paradox of a double-coded event.

5. CONCLUSION

Attempting to define the nature of Internet-based live performance work with dance elements, three issues need be addressed:

1　WHAT IS THE MEDIUM THE ARTIST IS WORKING WITH? It is important to clarify where the artists stand in terms of different materialities they are interacting with, different processes they are adopting and different techniques they are applying to their selected media. There is also the issue of 'perspective' which is about priorities and therefore about having the option to select different 'packages' of possibilities and limitations.

2　HYBRIDITY. In the juxtaposition/collaboration/synthesis of dance and technology new notions of time, space and dynamics and unprecedented interactive relationships between theory and practice have become possible. The body re-defines what technology is, technology makes possible new conceptions of dance. A combination of hybrid performing bodies and hybrid bodies of work draws new meanings out of the virtual, the physical and the material, different physicalities in the virtual, different virtualities in new materials.

3　SPACE. Space is re-configured through communication, collaboration, networks, exchanges based on a multiplicity of virtual and material means. There is an unavoidable multidimensionality in both the literal and metaphorical articulation of space. A conception of space which fundamentally occurs through time-processes in events which incorporate live transmission of data is one of the most intriguing. This is an articulation of space in constant flux, materials in a permanent state of transformation which evolve through endless stages of their own processes of re-organisation as they travel back and forth, creating points of contact and intimate interaction between remote locations, feeding the moment and the time, persistently shifting space through time frames.

Section 4: Glossary and Bibliography
4.1: Glossary
by Mark Batty

(Italicised words indicate a reference within the glossary)

32-bit/16-bit	The number of *bits* of information that an *operating system* requires to have flowing in order to run a certain *application*, 32-bit being the more advanced and demanding on the computer. This also has a bearing on the construction of the computer's *CPU* (Central Processing Unit). The Pentium *CPU*, for example, easily runs 32-bit *applications* because the wires that hold all the pieces together (its *bus*) are big enough to allow 32 *bits* of *digital* information to flow through at a time. 486, 386 *processors* and below weren't big enough because they were designed to handle 16 *bits* at a time.
Access provider	See *ISP*.
Acrobat Reader	An Adobe *software* product, available in a *freeware* version, that permits the *downloading*, viewing and printing of files (in 'portable document format') from the *web* in their original format. See *PDF*.
A.I.	See *Artificial Intelligence*.
Angle brackets	Used in *HTML* to differentiate between text to be seen on screen and 'text' embedded as instruction to the *browser* to indicate how the text should appear on screen. For example, <B>angle</B> has 'open' and 'close' instructions for bold type in angle brackets to instruct the browser to display the word 'angle' in bold.
ANSI	American National Standards Institute. The place that sets standards for *data* communications systems such as the *Internet*.
AppleShare	Apple Computer's *network* system that allows many different *users* to attach to one central computer, or *server*.
Applet	A very small *application* that serves one simple function.
Application	See *programme*.
Architecture	Used in a computing context to refer usually to a specifically developed and/or customised *hardware/platform/software* environment created for a specific project or task. Also used to

refer to the structuring and placing of information within *virtual* 'space' on a *web page*.

Artificial Intelligence *Software* that is 'intelligent', or that lends 'intelligence' to a machine or computer. 'Intelligence' might be deemed to be the computational part of the ability to solve problems and achieve goals.

ASCII American Standard Code for Information Interchange. This is the character set for figures and numbers, including many accented letters, represented in *binary* code. ASCII is the standard agreed manner in which characters are represented *digitally* by almost all *wordprocessor*s and other *applications*, providing a basic compatibility between them as far as text is concerned. The reason it is still difficult to transfer documents between different *wordprocessor*s, even for example *Windows* based ones, is because of all the embedded codes for tabs, paragraphs, spaces, page size, headers, footnotes etc. that differ from *software* to *software*.

ASP Active Server Pages. A *programming* tool based on Visual Basic (See *VBA*). ASP generates *HTML* pages (*web pages*) using any inputted information and is useful in the compilation of, for example, bibliographies published online, or such like.

Attachment It is possible to send any kind of document (a *wordprocessed* document, an image, a *spreadsheet*, a *database*) as an attachment to *an e-mail* message. How to use this facility will depend upon the *e-mail software* you are using, which all differ in the same way that *wordprocessing software* products differ. Often there can be problems with decoding the attachment when it is received – though this can sometimes be avoided by specifying clearly what kind of document is being sent to the *e-mail software* at the point of sending.

Author The creator of a piece of *software* or of a *web site*.

Avatar From the Sanscrit for the incarnation of Godhead, an avatar is the 'body' you 'wear' in a virtual community – an animated, articulated representation of a human which represents you, the user, in any virtual environment. Some of the more sophisticated chat rooms provide the facility to 'chat' over the Net via the visual representation of interacting human forms.

AVI Audio/Video Interleaved. Microsoft's format for encoding pictures and sound for *digital* transmission, and therefore the *extension* for files of this kind.

Background printing Being able to print a document without having to wait until it is completed before being able to use your computer again. *Windows* uses Print Manager to look after the printing of a document in background, allowing you to continue working while the printing takes place.

Back up   Making an identical copy of a file or files and storing it in a different place. Just in case.

Bad sector   A fault on a *floppy* or *hard disk*. Disks are divided into tracks and sectors where a sector is the smallest amount of the disk which can be written to or read from. A bad sector means that the disk surface is defective or damaged at this particular point and the drive cannot read from this part of the disk. There are, however, many sectors on the disk and it may be possible to rectify the problem by using the *Windows* '95 'disk tools', including 'Scandisk'.

Bandwidth   Measured in Megabytes (see *Bytes*), bandwidth describes the capacity (and by implication the speed) of a line that carries *digital* information from computer to computer across the *Internet*. The more 'traffic' (*TCP/IP* 'vehicles' – see *TCP/IP*), the faster this will flow if the 'roads' are wider.

Beta   The beta version of a new piece of *software* is one in the penultimate stage of its creation, and in the final phase of the pre-release testing cycle. It is often possible to *download* beta versions of experimental *software* from the *WWW* as often *software* companies need outside *users* to provide feedback for final revisions to a product.

BIOS   Basic Input/Output System. A very simple piece of *software* that the computer uses to wake itself up. When you switch on, the computer activates the BIOS *programme* to test all its components and see what kind of computer it is. It will beep (to say 'I'm alive!') and check the A: *drive* for a *system disk* (the evolutionary equivalent of the appendix, as computers used to start the operating system – see *DOS* – from a *floppy disk* – remember those old BBCs?) It will then find its *operating system* on the *hard disk* and finish *booting up*, leaving you to either log in to a *network*, key in a command or begin working in your *GUI* environment.

Binary   The manner in which a computer counts (see *Bit*). The decimal counting system is based around the number ten so the number 234 is made up of $2x10^2 + 3x10^1 + 4x10^0$ (or 200+30+4). In the binary counting system the number 2 is central and its figures can only contain a 0 or a 1 – so the binary number 1001 is made up of $1x2^3 + 0x2^2 + 0x2^1 + 1x2^0$ (or in other words 8+0+0+1, or 9 in decimal). Counting to five in binary becomes: 1 – 10 – 11 – 100 – 101. Another good reason for our having opposable thumbs!

Bit   BInary digiT. The smallest unit of information in a computer, either on or off, represented in binary as either 1 or 0.

BMP   The *extension* for a bitmap file, an image made up of little dots and stored *digitally*.

Booting up

From an old American phrase to do with pulling up your own boot strings (as opposed to being tied to apron strings). Booting up is the computer scratching itself after waking up and running a self-test before activating the *operating system*. A *networked* computer, on booting, is likely to link into the network and request your *username* and password.

Bookmarks

In Netscape *browsers*, once you have found a page on the *WWW* that you would like to return to, the *software* provides the facility to 'bookmark' the page. In Microsoft's Internet Explorer these are referred to as 'Favorites'.

BPS

Bits Per Second. The way in which the speed of a *modem* is measured referring to the number of *digital* 'bits' flow through it each second. The higher the BPS the better though the speed of information sending and receiving is also dependent upon the *bandwidth* of any line it must flow through (see *Bandwidth* and *ISDN*).

Browser

A form of *software* used for viewing pages on the *WWW*. Mosaic was the first widely available browser. Netscape Navigator and Microsoft Internet Explorer are the two most widely used browsers (both available as *freeware* to individual *users*), though there are others. As well as permitting you to view *web pages*, browser software comes with *Usenet* and *e-mail* facilities, making them useful ways of utilising these three aspects of the *Internet*. Browsers can be made more flexible by the addition of *plug-ins*.

Buffer

A section of the computer where *data* is stored 'at the ready' before being used. Buffering allows time for an *application* to fix differences in *bit* rates, creating compensatory spaces that allow things to flow with more fluidity in front of you.

Bugs

Glitches in *programming* that cause errors to occur when *software* is running.

Bulletin Boards

The *virtual* versions of these everyday objects that carry pinned masses of paper on our walls. The *Usenet* is a collection of specific bulletin boards, but these also form a part of numerous *web sites* as separate pages which contain updated information for those who frequently refer to that particular *site*.

Burn

When a *CD-ROM* is copied onto another one, or created afresh, we speak of the files being 'burned' onto it.

Burst

To send *data* (between components within a computer) in a large package all at once rather than in small *bits* over a longer time.

Bus

All the components of your computer; the *mouse*, the *monitor*, the printer, the *processor*, the *hardware* cards, the *memory* and so on are all connected by wires. This system of wires is called the bus.

Bytes

A measurement of the amount of *digitally* stored or carried information, used to measure memory and document size. To be precise a byte is a grouping of binary digits representing information, a set of 8 *bits* making up a manageable unit of memory. The capacity of a *floppy disk* is measured in kilobytes (KB) (one kilobyte = 1024 bytes) and a *hard disk* in megabytes (MB) or gigabytes (GB) (one megabyte = 1024 kilobytes). A high capacity *hard disk* is necessary for those who wish to store numerous image (or similar memory-hungry) files but less necessary for those working solely on text documents; it will not significantly affect performance. It is the *RAM* capacity of a computer that affects the speed and efficiency of the machine. 32 megabytes of *RAM* is usually adequate for most simple computing tasks.

Cache

This is a *memory* section that holds *data* while the *CPU* is working on it (see *RAM*). *Browsers* such as Netscape also maintain a cache of files as they are displayed for you off the *WWW*. These are used when you want to go back through *web pages* you have already accessed and saves the *browser* having to call them up again from their original location.

CAD

Computer-Aided Design. The generic term for a specific type of *software* product that is used to construct and manipulate theoretical models *virtually*.

Capture

One can 'capture' a still image from a video using certain software. A 'screen capture' (i.e. creating an image of what you see currently on your PC screen) can be made by pressing 'ALT' + 'Prt Sc' in *Windows*. This can then be inserted into any document.

Card

A piece of hardware that performs a specific function. This slots into an expansion slot, which is connected to the *PC's motherboard*, and expands the functionality of the computer. *Ethernet* cards and sound cards are two examples.

Chat Rooms

Special *web sites* that contain individual pages ('rooms') in which you can 'chat' with random surfers or arrange rendezvous. The 'chat' takes the form of inputting lines of text, often with the option of complementary 'emotion' signifiers, and waiting for a typed response. These may be *HTML* pages, or more efficient and speedy *Java* pages. Some suppliers are now experimenting with 'voice mail' *applications* similar to conference telephone calls.

CD-ROM

A form of 'read only' *data* storage (see *ROM*). A Compact *disk* has a massive storage capacity compared to a *floppy disk* and has become a standard way of offering *software*. The speed of a CD-ROM drive will dictate how fast information can be read from a CD-ROM placed in it.

CGA
Colour Graphics Adapter. PC computer screens could originally only display monochrome text on a black background. Graphics adapters were then made available such as IBM's CGA which was capable of creating graphics and text in colour at low *resolution* – 300×200 *pixels* with 16 colours per *pixel* possible. This made the *GUI* possible and greater *user-friendliness*.

Click
To activate an *icon*, a *menu* or any item on screen by pointing a *mouse* cursor at it and clicking on the *mouse* key. The left button is the most commonly used one, but the right button can have specific uses within different *applications* and most often provides a *drop-down menu* pertinent to wherever the cursor is placed.

CMC
Computer mediated communication.

.com
(pronounced 'dot com'). 'Dot com' refers to the practice of (originally) commercial US *web sites* indicating their nature within their *web* address with this suffix (www.microsoft.com, for example). The practice in the UK was often a '.co.uk' suffix. 'Dot com' has entered popular vocabulary as an indicator of *Internet* presence (of a company or organisation) or of *web* activity in general. See *Domain*, *URL* and *WWW*.

Compressed files
Large files that have been reduced in capacity in order to allow them to be *downloaded* over the *Internet* more speedily, either using *FTP* or a *web browser*, and which require decompression *software* in order to be used. Unzip is one such *programme* for the Mac and Winzip does the trick for the PC.

Computer
A device which processes and stores information *digitally*.

Computer literacy
The ability confidently and competently to make good or optimum use of the facilities that computers provide.

CPU
Central Processing Unit. See *Processor*.

Crash
When a computer seizes up and will no longer respond to commands, it has crashed. This is usually not your fault!

Cursor
A blinking line indicating where typed text will appear. The pointer that moves across the screen when you move the *mouse* can also be referred to as a cursor, though it isn't.

Cut and Paste
To delete a selection of text from a document and place it elsewhere in the same, or a different, document. It is possible to cut and paste from *e-mail* and *web pages* into documents, making this a handy function to master.

Cyberspace
In William Gibson's book, 'Neuromancer', Cyberspace is defined as 'an infinite artificial world where humans navigate in information-based space', and 'the ultimate computer-human interface'. This is a place of 'virtual reality' where information flows down cables in digital '*bits*'. The information does not exist in any tangible form anywhere but is accessed by computers tapping into other computers connected by servers,

allowing the information (text, graphics, video, software etc.) to flow wherever it is beckoned. The human conceptual mind deals with this by creating an imaginary space where all the information is stored. This library/shopping mall/theatre/ meeting room is Cyberspace.

Data   Information that is collected, stored or processed systematically.

Database   A *programme* that helps to gather together information, such as bibliographic material or lists of addresses, usually in tabular form, and make it more easily accessible, sortable and searchable.

Database engine A *programme* which performs the database management functions on *data* held in a *database*. That is to say it can manipulate, add, delete, search, select and store *data* following simple *user* commands.

Decompress   see *Compressed files*

Default   Any pre-set value which will be used by a *programme* if you don't choose another option in its place. *Windows* default colours are blue and grey but you can adapt these to suit your whim. A *wordprocessor* will always assume you intend to print on upright (portrait) A4 paper with standard margins around your text – these are default values.

Defragmenting   When you've had enough of all your books, texts and papers cluttering up your desk you might decide to sort through them and leave them in a tidy pile on one side of the desk. This is what the *PC* does when you ask it to defragment your *hard disk*. When a file is created it is left any-old-where on the *hard disk*. When the disk is defragmented the computer collects all these files together and deposits them in one area, leaving a nice clean collection of empty sectors on the hard disk, ready for more information. Defragmenting the hard disk every two months or so (if you use a *stand alone*) is good computer health procedure. *Windows* '95 and '98 give you this option from within 'disk tools'.

Desktop computer A full sized computer with a 14", 15", 16" or even 17" *monitor* and flat or *tower* casing. It may be a *stand-alone* or it may be connected to a *network*.

Desktop publishing *Software* that assists in creating sophisticated documents including complicated page designs, detailed illustrations, and camera-ready typefaces.

Dialogue box   A way that Graphic User Interfaces (*GUIs* such as *Windows* or the *Mac* Desktop) use to ask us for what we want in a specific situation. For example, when you open a *word processor* and select 'open' from the file menu a dialogue box will pop up so that you can specify which document you wish to open. You might then select which *drive* or *directory* (folder) to look in or what type of file you want.

Digital

Computers carry out all their operations using *binary*, describing information in a series of switches that are either on or off (1 or 0). As all information is dealt with using these two digits, we talk of the digitalisation of text, images, video etc. when these things are to be stored or processed by computers. 'Digital' is also commonly used adjectivally to describe processes or facilities which involve the collection or manipulation of *digitised* information such as 'digital libraries' or 'digital video' or even 'digital culture'.

Digitise

To convert any text, video or audio material into a *digital* file – to reproduce in *digital* media.

Directory

Files (whether our own documents or those pertaining to *software*) are kept in specific directories (known as Folders in Windows '95 and the *Mac*). These can be used, created and manipulated in order to sort our documents sensibly (using 'file manager' in *Windows* or 'Explorer' in Windows '95). You can create new directories and move files from one to another. Avoid moving *software* files though as this can be disastrous.

Directory tree

A pictorial representation of the way information is stored in *directories* and their subdirectories on your *hard disk*. 'Windows Explorer' in *Windows* will provide such an image and permit you to cut and 'prune' it.

Domain

The 'home turf' of any *web site*. The domain of the *SCUDD web site* is the Nottingham Trent University's *server*, as denoted in the root (art.ntu.ac.uk) of its *URL*: http://art.ntu.ac.uk/scudd/ Commercially, *web* domains can be chosen and registered to be easily remembered, such as http://www.sainsburys.co.uk/

DOS

Disk Operating System. The system that 'operates' the hard disk. When we speak of DOS we are referring to the old Microsoft operating system *software* though, of course, all computers have a disk operating system (AmiDos for the Amiga, for example). The operating system is very basic *software* that must be in place before a computer can do anything and on top of which all other *software* runs. Before Graphic User Interfaces (*GUIs* – that use *icons* and menus to access programmes and functions) and 'What You See is What You Get' (*WYSIWYG*) word processors, DOS was the system that required commands typed in at a *prompt* using the keyboard to perform any operation. It is still sitting under *Windows*, which, being more *user-friendly* behaves as an interpreter, translating our commands into DOS for us. Of course, the *Mac* had all this stitched up years ago, and uses much less memory in the process. Before *Windows* (or running despite it) software was written to run in DOS (you might type 'word' at the DOS *prompt*, for example, to open DOS version of the 'Word' word processor).

The disadvantage of these was that it was frequently unclear what the final layout of a document might be.

Dot com   See *.com*.

Double-click   To click the *mouse* button twice in quick succession.

Download   To transfer files from elsewhere to your own space (to a *hard disk*, *floppy disk* or *server* memory space). The term is used most often in reference to the way in which files (documents or *programmes*) can be accessed transferred from a *remote* computer to your own via the *Internet*.

Dragging   Clicking the *mouse* and, without letting go, moving its pointer to another part of the document. In this way you can select specific pieces of text which can then be copied and pasted in another document, or deleted, or moved by using a *drag and drop* motion.

Drag and drop   To take a selection of text, or an image, and – by holding down the *mouse* key with the pointer over the selection – shifting it to another place in the same document.

Dreamweaver   A Macromedia *software* product that aids in the authoring of *web pages* and the management of *web sites*. It permits the *user* to maintain an overview of a complex site, and to *upload* updates of the *site* onto the *web*.

Drive   The space where a disk is kept and read or written to. The A: or B: drive on a *PC* holds the extractable *floppy disk*, the C: drive contains the permanent *hard disk* and the D: drive is commonly used for the *CD-ROM* drive. On a *network server* other drives will exist, their use depending on the policy of those who run the *server*. Commonly the M: drive is where *users* are allocated memory space to save their documents.

Drop-down menu   A *menu* of available options provided by an *application* when, using the *mouse* (or often the ALT key with the *navigation keys*), you click on the *menu's* title (usually found on the top border of an *application's* 'window') Also a method of selecting options on a *web page* or a *web* form. In a *wordprocessor*, for example, clicking on the 'File' on the menu bar will provide a drop-down menu offering a selection of functions that might be carried out on the file presently open. In a *web page*, you might come across a drop-down menu offering a list of links off that page, or offering a selection of *data* to input into a form (destinations on a flight-booking page, for example).

DVD, DVD-ROM   Digital Versatile *Disk* (or Digital Video *Disk*). A *multimedia* format that holds video, audio and computer *data*. These can be 'played' in video-like boxes attached to your television or in DVD-ROM drives built into personal computers. In appearance very similar to *CD-ROMs*, DVD *disks* have higher storage capacity, up to 17GB of *data* (compared to roughly 650MB on a CD). See *Bytes*.

E-	An abbreviation of *Electronic* and used as a prefix to indicate this. See *Electronic*.
EGA	Enhanced Graphics Adapter. An improvement on the *CGA*. Allowed the computer *monitor* to display more dots per screen permitting 400×300 *pixels* at 16 colours or 300×200 at 256 colours.
Electronic	Used adjectivally to describe *digital* artefacts, and might often be replaced by '*virtual*' or '*digital*'. We speak of electronic articles on the *web*, for example, and most commonly of electronic mail. Electronic is commonly abbreviated to the prefix 'e-', and so we hear of e-journals, e-supplements, e-publishing and of course *e-mail*:
E-Mail	Electronic mail sent using the *Internet*. You can only send e-mail from a computer with a *modem* or one which is connected to a network with an *Internet* facility. There are different types of e-mail *software programmes*, 'Pegasus mail' being a popular one because it is available as *Freeware* from the *WWW* to individual *users*. Other common programmes include Simeon and Eudora, and e-mail is integral to certain *software* packages such as Outlook. E-mail is useful not only for passing memos internally, or for contacting people nationally and internationally cheaply and quickly (within seconds), but also as a way of passing documents for others to read as an *attachment*.
E-Mail lists	It is possible to subscribe to various e-mail lists set up by or originating in different organisations or interest groups. Anyone who mails to the list has a copy of their message posted to every subscriber.
Encryption	One of many methods of 'translating' a file into a hard-to-crack code for added security during *Internet* transfer.
End-user	The audience, the 'market', the people for whom a certain product/*web site*/activity is intended.
Entry level	As the computer market continues to rush on, what is 'standard' is continually shifting and the 'entry level' that some may speak of is the minimum specification you might consider when purchasing a computer.
Ethernet	One of the two most frequently used ways to configure (set up and connect) a *network* of computers. Token ring is the other. Adding an ethernet card to the *motherboard* of a *stand-alone PC* gives it the capacity of running as a *networked* computer.
Executable	An executable file is any file that will carry out specific tasks when 'opened' and will commonly have the 'exe' *extension* in *DOS* based systems. So, for example, when you open up *Windows* you have activated the windows.exe file.
Extension	*DOS* (and consequently any *Windows application* before Windows '95) has specific rules for the way in which any files

created can be named. A file name in a *DOS*-based system (*PCs*) has two parts; the root and the extension separated by a full-stop e.g. myfile.doc (the root has a maximum of eight letters, the extension just three). The root is the name the *user* chooses to give his/her file, the extension can also be used to identify files but *DOS* and *Windows programmes* use them to identify certain types of files. For example, the 'doc' extension is used by the 'Word' *wordprocessor*, the 'txt' extension by the 'Notepad' *application*, the 'wps' extension is used by 'Works' etc. Windows '95 got rid of the need for extensions and allows the *user* to have much larger file names (though it secretly converts everything to *DOS* itself).

FAQ

Frequently Asked Questions – very often, when you access a *web site* on the *WWW* for information, there will be a FAQ page, which you should read through before contacting the authors for additional information. This is part of the courtesy quaintly known as '*netiquette*'.

Field

When speaking of how *data* might be collected in *databases*, or using feedback forms on *web pages*, for example, we speak of collecting information in pertinent fields. Collecting Surnames together in a 'surname' field, for instance, would require that such a field be established within the *software* that will be sorting inputted *data*.

Firewall

A kind of electronic fence around a *web site* or an *intranet* that stops non-subscribers or non-employees from accessing the information and facilities installed there.

FireWire

A connection for digital video devices such as digital camcorders. A composite of six wires: two for power, two for *data* and two for synchronisation. Also known as an *i.link*.

FirstClass

A Soft Arc *server software* product that gives a company or organisation facilities for *Internet* and *intranet* capabilities without reliance on an *access provider*.

Flame

To send abusive or inappropriate *e-mails*.

Flash

A Macromedia *software* product that allows the delivery of highly *compressed interactive* animations and audio on *web pages*.

Floppy Disk

A form of portable *data* storage – an electronic briefcase. The standard floppy disk is now the hard cased 3.5" disk which is neither floppy nor disk-shaped (until you crack it open). Previously, there was the 5.25" floppy that was cased in paper. Floppies most often fit into the A: or B: *drive* in the front of your computer. (The C: *drive* is the internal *hard disk* and the D: drive is now commonly the *CD-ROM* or *DVD-ROM drive*). There are two drive letters allocated to the floppy because for a while computers had *drives* for both the 5.25" (A:) and the 3.5" (B:) disks before the latter became standard.

Font	That which we would otherwise refer to as typeface.
Format	Verb: To format a *floppy disk* is to prepare it to receive and store material in the appropriate manner (using the *DOS* system for example, as opposed to the *Mac* or vice versa) The Mac calls this 'initialising'. Disks are usually available pre-formatted. Noun: when we speak of the format of a file we are most often talking about what system (PC or Mac?) or what *wordprocessor* (Word or Wordperfect?) the document has been produced using. Most *wordprocessors* provide a facility by which you can make a copy of your document in a different format (try the 'save as...' function).
Frames	Some *web pages* are actually composed of two or three individual *web pages*, arranged in 'frames'. You might often come across a 'navigation frame', providing links to key areas of a *site*, that will remain on screen as you browse the site of which it is a part. Some apparently framed sites actually create the impression by using *tables* instead of frames.
Freeware	*Software* which costs nothing to buy or use.
FrontPage	See *Microsoft FrontPage*.
FTP	File Transfer Protocol. An old way of storing and transferring files using the *Internet*. A great deal of *shareware* and *freeware* is available on the *Internet* using FTP (which is what happens when you *download* anything from the *Internet*, whether it be from a *WWW* page or a FTP site). An FTP site begins with ftp:// (as opposed to *web* addresses that begin with http://) and can be accessed using a browser just like any *web page*. FTP sites contain directories of files that can be *downloaded*. FTP is popular for transferring large files and these are often '*compressed*' to save time and money. To decompress these you first need to download the appropriate '*decompressing*' or 'unzipping' *software* and *install* it on your computer following instructions provided (see *ZIP* and *Plug-in*). The Netscape *browser* usually intervenes to help you find this *software*. It can be a bit of a fiddle but can prove useful. FTP details, a guide and questions answered can be accessed on the *Internet* at http://www.faqs.org/faqs/ftp-list/faq/
Gateway	For example, Common Gateway Interface (CGI). A piece of *software* that allows two computers (or different systems within a computer) to communicate with each other.
Geek	See *Nerd*.
GIF	Graphical Interchange Format. An alternative to the *BMP* (bitmap) as a manner of storing images digitally.
Gopher	Special *software* developed at the University of Minnesota that provided access to resources on the *Internet* before the popularity of *browsers*.

GoLive   An Adobe *software* product for web-authoring and *site* maintenance.

GPF   General Protection Fault. A very frustrating and all too frequent occurrence for many *users* is when a *PC crashes* or freezes in the middle of some task. A general protection fault is usually caused by a conflict in one of your configuration files (either config.sys or autoexec.bat) and is therefore only fixable by the extremely *computer literate*. In most cases you can choose to 'ignore' the problem but often it is best to cash in your chips, close the *application* that was running, losing any unsaved information and *boot up* the computer again.

GUI   Graphic User Interface. Any 'interface' between you and the computer's abilities that enables you to tell the machine what to do by using *icons* and images (and a *mouse* to manipulate these). *Windows* is such an environment, and the *Mac* had always used this form of interface.

Hacker   Someone so *computer literate* they are able to 'hack' into computers (i.e. access and/or manipulate *data* held in them) usually employing a cunning ability to bypass or override password protection and other security strategies. Hackers often work at a distance physically from their target computers by abusing the facilities of the *Internet*.

Hard Copy   The printed version of any document created using a computer *programme*, such as a *wordprocessor*. We used to refer to these as papers, pamphlets and books.

Hard Disk   A permanent disk within most computers (certainly all
(or hard drive or fixed disk) *PCs* and *Macs*) where *software* and/or your documents may be stored.

Hardware   All the stuff you have physically manifest in front of you, or which sits inside these components. Your printer, keyboard, *mouse*, *monitor*, tower etc. are all computer hardware.

Hotlink   A *link* on a *web page* to another *web page*. In Netscape *Navigator*, private hotlinks are called *bookmarks*. See *link*.

HTML   Hypertext Mark-up Language. The language used for writing basic *web pages* (see *WWW*). A list of basic parameters indicate to a *web browser* how text and images should appear and be laid out on the screen. To view the HTML version of a *web page* select the 'view' menu on the top line of your *browser* and choose 'document source' (in Netscape Navigator) or 'source' (in Internet Explorer). *Web pages* invariably have the html or htm *extension* to indicate that they are html documents. *Web pages* can be authored ('written') either using HTML grammar in a simple text file or by using software packages that translate your instructions into HTML. HoT MeTaL, Dreamweaver and MS Internet Assistant are three such packages.

HTTP   Hypertext Transfer *Protocol*. Addresses of sites on the *WWW*
                                           begin with these letters, indicating that the page concerned is a
                                           web page and not, for example, an *FTP* index.

Hypertext
(see also *HTML*).   Hypertext is also a term used to refer to 'embedded' text that
                                           pops up when you click on a word to offer further detail or
                                           clarification. *Users* of *Windows'* Help pages or Encarta will be
                                           familiar with this.

Hyperlinks   See *links*.
Hypermedia   The various *digital* and *online* media, such as *CD-ROM*, the
                                           Internet, *webcasting* etc.

Icons   The tiny pictures that represent actions or programmes, usually
                                           indicating facilities (within *software*) or *pathways* (on the *web*).

I.mac   The latest '*Internet* ready' series of Apple Macintosh computers.
Information superhighway   See *Internet*.
Initialising   See *Format*.
Install   To place *software* onto your *hard disk* so that you can
                                           subsequently make use of it.

Integrated package   A *programme* that performs two or more tasks. Most commonly
                                           this might involve *wordprocessor*, *database* and *spreadsheet*
                                           software all in one package. Examples of this are MS-Works
                                           and Lotus 1-2-3.

Interactivity   A method of becoming involved with *software* that is dictated
                                           by the whim, interest or enthusiasms of the *user*. *Digital*
                                           encyclopaedias, games, *web sites* and some art *programming*
                                           involve interactivity in as much as they provide a non-linear
                                           approach to viewing and accessing information.

Interface   Any type of point where two different things come together:
                                           you and a computer (see *GUI*); a computer and another computer
                                           (see *TCP/IP*); different communications systems.

Internet   A collection of computers interconnected globally, administered
                                           and controlled by nobody. There are several parts to the *Internet*:
                                           e-mail, *FTP*, newsgroups, The World Wide Web (*WWW*) and
                                           Telnet. You tap into the Internet via a *modem* which is attached
                                           to your computer or through the network server and use it to
                                           access files, information, or to send electronic messages with *e-
                                           mail*. The *modem* contacts the closest *Internet* host computer
                                           using a telephone or *ISDN* line. More often than not you view
                                           information from the *Internet* using a *browser*.

I/O Ports   Connectors that allow you to attach *peripherals*, such as *modems*
                                           or printers, to your computer.

i.link   See *FireWire*.
Intranet   A network within an organisation that uses *Internet* technology.
                                           An Intranet behaves exactly like the *Internet* in that you can
                                           retrieve pages from *servers*, the difference is that it is not part

of the *Internet*, and cannot be accessed from outside the organisation. The beauty of the system is that all *data* can be stored centrally, allowing easier maintenance. Intranet based information systems are gradually replacing some traditional Client/Server type systems because of the ease of use of web-based *browser* interfaces.

ISP

Internet service provider. A company that provides access to the *Internet* to domestic or commercial *users*. BT, Demon, Which? Tesco.net, AOL and Compuserve are examples of these, all running different fee systems (you may pay a fixed monthly fee, or a fee per second *online*, or a combination of these two). Some providers charge a fixed monthly sum, some are 'pay as you use' or a combination of both, increasingly 'free' offers feature in the marketing.

ISDN

Integrated Services Digital Network. A much faster way of connecting to the *Internet* and an alternative to the standard telephone line. Most of the world's existing telephone network is already *digital*, with the exception of the line between the exchange and our homes or offices. By providing a *digital link* there too the whole network is *digital* and therefore much faster.

IT/I.T.

Information Technology. All computer related technology, including all *hardware* and *software*. 'Information', as essentially computers are processors of information (*data*).

Java

A supplementary language to *HTML* that is used to produce jazzier and funkier *web pages* (*HTML* being mostly limited to text and layout). Java functions by offering *object*-based 'packages' that the browser downloads when it comes across a page written in Java. These 'packages' are little *applications* (or '*applets*') that do tricks when they *download* and are 'read' by your *browser*, producing moving images and animated text.

Java Script

A *web* programming language very close to *Java* that permits greater interaction between a *web page* and its viewer.

JPEG

Joint Photographic Experts Group. An image format that compresses a *digitally* stored picture and is therefore less memory-hungry than, say, *GIF* files. The file *extension* for JPEG files is jpg.

LAN

Local Area *Network*. A collection of computers linked via a *TCP/IP network* to a nearby *server*. An *intranet* is an example of a LAN.

Laptop computer

As opposed to a *desktop computer*, a smaller, portable machine that most often has a *monitor* attached to, and which folds into, the keyboard.

LCD

Liquid Crystal Display. Used for the flat screens found on laptops.

Link

A connection between two *web pages*, either between those

kept on the same *site* or those kept on different *sites*. By clicking on a link using the *mouse* pointer you are automatically taken to the new page. You can retrace your steps by clicking on the *browser's* 'back' button on its *toolbar*.

LINUX
A *UNIX*-like *operating system* that was designed by Linus Torvalds at the University of Helsinki to provide *PC* users with a free or very low-cost *operating system* comparable to *UNIX* systems. Unlike Microsoft *Windows*, LINUX is extendible by contributors. LINUX is sometimes suggested as a possible publicly developed alternative to the desktop predominance of Microsoft *Windows*.

Log-in, Log-off, Log-on
Logging in or on is simply punching your metaphoric card when you first connect to your *network* – you are asking to be connected to the *server* computer to use its facilities. Logging off is the reverse. We also speak of 'logging on to the *Internet*'.

Load
Abbreviation of 'download', see *Download*.

Mac
The Apple Macintosh computer. After the market leading *PCs*, the Mac is the most popular form of computer and is arguably superior in design, *software* and usability. Frequently, those who have used a Mac prefer to stay with the machine but, until recently, the lack of compatibility with the *PCs* (produced by any number of companies based on the IBM model) has caused it to be left by the wayside to a degree.

Mainframe computer
The largest type of computer, and the first. Early mainframes often filled entire rooms with their tubes and tapes performing operations that today's least powerful machines wouldn't blink at.

Mark-up codes,
Mark-up language
Digital text appears on our screens in *wordprocessors*, in *Internet browsers* and from *DVD* and *CD-ROMs* without any mark-up codes visible. However, in order for text to appear, for example, indented, italicised, in paragraphs or in varying *fonts*, the author of the *digital* material will need to 'mark up' text with the codes that indicate to the viewing *software* how the text should appear. Collections of codes form these languages such as *HTML*.

Master
The primary copy of a document or collection of documents, or files. A master-disk might contain such a collection.

Memory
We speak of a computer's storage capacity as its memory, but also its capacity to hold information open whilst in use. See *bytes*, *RAM* and *ROM*.

Menu
A list of available options. These are often available as *drop-down menus* across the top border of an *application's* active 'window' on the screen.

Menu bar
The horizontal bar listing the available *menus* (such as 'file',

	'edit' or 'format') on screen when an *application* is active. Below this there are usually other bars, such as the *tool bar*.
Menu-driven options	Rather than expecting or requesting a *user* to input *data* (in a *dialogue box*, for example), menu-driven options within *software* or on the *web* allow the user to make choices from a series of menus.
Microsoft Access **(MS Access)**	A Microsoft *software* product that is primarily a *data* management tool (*database software*). Access has tools to enter, edit, and index *data* and to retrieve it via custom forms and reports. It also contains Visual Basic for Applications (See *VBA*).
Microsoft FrontPage **(MS FrontPage)**	A Microsoft *software* product that facilitates *web* design and *web site* management.
Microsoft PowerPoint **(MS PowerPoint)**	A Microsoft *software* product which aids in the creation of professional-looking presentations. PowerPoint handles text, outlines, drawings, graphics, and clip-art in the design of presentations and 'slide-shows'.
MIDI	Musical Instrument Digital Interface. A set of standards by which computers can work with other digital equipment, such as synthesisers and tape recorders, to record and play back sound.
Millennium problem	Computers run many *programmes* dependent on knowledge of the date and time. Many older computers were limited to recognising dates up to, but no further than, 31 December 1999. If these computers, including large *mainframes*, were not updated by the year 2000 the fear was that a great deal of havoc could have been let loose on world banking and military programming, to mention but a couple of areas that were thought in risk of serious trouble. Apple Macs were not affected by this problem.
Mirror	A copy (usually of *web sites*). A mirror site is a *web site* that is an identical copy of another site (often with or without the permission of the author).
Modem	MOdulator-DEModulator (which means the changing of *data* from digital to analogue – i.e. computer language to phone line language – and then back again). A piece of *hardware* which attaches to the computer (internally or externally) and provides a link to a telephone or *ISDN* line, allowing the computer to access the *Internet*. The speed of the modem is measured in bps (*bits* per second), a V32, for example, running at 9,600bps. The faster the modem the quicker *e-mail* is sent or received and the quicker *WWW* pages will *download*, and therefore the cheaper it is to run on your phone bill.

Monitor	The 'TV bit' of your computer. The screen.
Mother	The home, or base. A Mother site would be the original of any *mirror* sites. See *Mirror*.
Motherboard	The motherboard is to the *PC* what a foundation is to a house. The *CPU* and all elements of the computer are plugged into it and are interconnected through it. This is found within the flat or *tower* casing.
Mouse	Perhaps the smallest piece of the computer's visible *hardware*, the mouse is attached to the computer via a *port* and is used, like the keyboard, to pass the *user*'s instructions to the computer. Its most basic functions are to allow us to point at an area on the screen and activate screen buttons or *applications* with clicks of the mouse buttons, and to select text in a block (by *dragging* the *mouse*). It is also a way of accessing certain menus (try clicking the right button when certain *programmes* are open). Left-handed *users* can easily swap the functions of the two main *mouse* buttons by adapting the computer's set up.
MP3	MPeg 1 Audio Layer 3 (the abbreviation MP3 is easier!) A compression form that permits the storage of audio without using excessive *memory*. MP3 files are becoming the standard for storing and downloading music on the *Internet*. MP3 players (the size of small walkmans) can be bought onto which *downloaded* files can be stored and listened to.
MPEG	Motion Picture Experts Group. A file format used for making, viewing, and transferring both digital audio and digital video files.
Multimedia	Usually pertaining to a *format*, such as a *DVD-ROM disk*, or any *IT* experience, that involves simultaneous access and use of more than one media – video and audio together, for example. Also used to describe any experience or performance involving such technologies.
Multitasking	Using your computer to run two or more *programmes* at once. You might, for example, open two documents simultaneously to edit between them and need a *spreadsheet* open to refer to. *Macs* have had little trouble *multitasking*, though it was not until *Windows* '95 that *PCs* became happy with the chore.
Navigate	Used often in relation to *Internet* experiences or *CD-ROM* facilities, as these often provide non-linear *pathways* for accessing information or entertainment.
Navigation keys	These are a collection of ten keys that are found between the character keys and the number keys on 'advanced' keyboards (which are now standard – previously these keys had been combined with the number keys and used by taking the number lock off). They consist of four arrow keys that will move a cursor up, down, to the left and right in a document and a group

of more specific keys: The 'Home' key (that will usually take you to the beginning of a line of text); the 'End' (that will take you to the end of the line); the 'PgUp' key (that will take you a page – or a screen display – further up the document); the 'PgDn' key (that will take you a page further down); the 'Delete' key (that deletes characters ahead of the cursor or any selected text) and the 'Insert' key (that functions in different ways according to the *programme*, but can be used to paste a copied selection). These keys have greater powers when used in conjunction with others. For example, pressing the 'Control' (ctrl) key and the reverse arrow will move you back a word at a time, and pressing the 'control' key with the 'home' key will usually take you to the beginning of the document.

Navigator   A Netscape *software* product, available in *freeware* versions. A *browser* for viewing *web pages*. See *browser*.

Nerd   Someone so unfortunate as to believe that all conversations might productively revolve around computing and —*IT* issues. Interestingly, only a nerd might know that the word derives from the 1950 Dr. Seuss book 'If I Ran the Zoo' from which: 'And then, just to show them, I'll sail to Ka-Troo – And Bring Back an It-Kutch, a Preep and a Proo – A Nerkle, a Nerd, and a Seersucker, too!' See *Geek*.

Net   A common abbreviation of the *Internet*.

Netiquette   *Internet* etiquette, including basic decent behaviour such as: not sending junk messages; not *flaming*; not *spamming*; not violating copyright; staying on topic in newsgroups.

Network   A collection of computers within a building or across a campus that all access the same *software* held by the *server*. When you log on to a network the *programmes* you use are not necessarily held within the memory of the computer in front of you but are held and administered centrally.

Notepad   An extremely basic *wordprocessing application* that is an integral part of all versions of Microsoft's *Windows*.

Object   A file that contains not only *data* but also the *application* that operates upon that *data*.

OCR   Optical Character Recognition. The machine-reading of typed or even hand-written texts by a scanner. *Software* then 'translates' the dark and light areas of the scanned material into letters and numbers and creates a text document from the scanned material.

Off-line   To work 'off-line' means to use your computer as a *stand-alone* and not use the *software* available to it when connected to a *network* via your local *server*. The opposite, 'online', is self-explanatory but is also used to describe being connected to the *Internet*.

Online	Connected to the *Internet*. See also *Off-line*.
Online scholarship	'Distance learning' facilitated using web-based techniques.
OOP	Object Oriented Program. A large *programme* made up of smaller *objects*.
Operating System	*Software* that translates your commands to the computer. See *DOS*.
Orphan	A *web page* which remains on the *web* but has no links to it, or has had its links from the main site severed. Similarly, a file created by a *programme* but which remains on your computer after that *programme* has been deleted might be deemed an 'orphan'.
Page Mill	An Adobe *software* product that facilitates *web page* design.
Pathway	When accessing linked pages on the *WWW* or when *navigating* through the information on a *DVD* or *CD-ROM* any *user* might choose distinct routes through the available material. These are commonly referred to as 'pathways'.
PC	Personal Computer. Technically, this term is used only for IBM and IBM-compatible computers (clones), all of which dominate the vast majority of the market. Other computers include the Apple Mac, the Amigas and the old Amstrads – these are not PCs (though, confusingly, you might consider them to be personal computers, with a small p and c), and, of these, Mac is the market leader. To make things more difficult, Apple Macintosh produce PowerPCs. The difference stems historically from the decision by Apple to produce machines that were complete in themselves and did not require or encourage the *user* to maintain or adapt them. IBM, on the other hand, produced a computer that could be made up of different components, according to the requirements of the *user*. IBM also used *DOS*, and then *Windows* applications, before Bill Gates went his own way with these products to create the Microsoft empire. Consequently, Microsoft products (such as *Windows*) run on PCs and not on other forms of computers, which have their own operating systems (see *DOS*).
PCI, (PCI Bus)	Peripheral Component Interconnect. A method of transferring *data* within your computer. Integrated into the *motherboard* of your *PC* is a system of wires known as the *bus* which connects all the various components (see *Bus*). When the original *bus* design – constructed to cope with the operating speed of the average *processor* (originally 4.77mhz) – proved too outdated to work alongside far more speedy modern *processors* and computer components, a much faster system of connecting wires was needed to keep up. PCI *bus* was Intel's answer and is now considered standard.
PDF	Portable Document Format. Technology which permits you to

	download, view and print documents from the *web* in their original form, and not as 'text only' files. See *Acrobat Reader*.
Peripheral	Any device attached to your computer, such as a printer.
Personal Web Server	Microsoft's Personal Web Server (PWS) (free as part of NT Option Pack 4 and also included in the Windows '98 CD). A development platform for *web applications* and good for developing and testing Active Server Pages (*ASP*) applications.
Photoshop	An Adobe *software* product. Image manipulation *software*, useful for working on *digitised* photographs or any other image.
PICT	A less common image file *format*. See *BMP*, *JPEG*, *GIF* and *TIFF*.
Pipeline burst cache	The *memory* of most *PCs* comes in three tiers. First, fastest but smallest is the internal *cache* that is actually within the *processor* itself. The *processor* can access the *data* in this memory virtually immediately. Next comes the external *cache*, which is usually on the *motherboard*, and which is bigger than internal *cache* but four times slower. Finally, there's the computer's main *memory* (in *RAM* chips), which is bigger and slower still. When the *processor* needs *data* it attempts to find it at the fastest level. When it can't find what it needs in its internal *cache*, it looks in external *cache*, and so on to the main memory until it succeeds. If the *data* exists externally to the *processor* it is sent in a rapid burst (a 'burst fill') of four or more 'packages'. Pipelined burst cache is a form of *cache* that operates by sending one package of *data* as it prepares subsequent ones which are then sent simultaneously (hence 'pipelining'). It is therefore faster than forms of *cache* that send *data* bit by bit.
Pixel	A *digitally* stored element of a picture represented by one dot on the screen. A standard *VGA* screen has 640 horizontal dots by 480 vertical dots. See *Resolution*.
Plasma screen	Monitors that make use of Gas plasma technology to permit the design of flat screens that can, amongst other things, be wall-mounted.
Platform	When people talk of the platform they use they are referring to the environment they use on their computer, such as *Windows* '95. This term is also used for describing the different games consoles (Sega, Nintendo etc.), computers that run only games *programmes*.
Plug and Play	Being able to take any card from any manufacturer, install it in an expansion slot in your *PC* (so called because they provide for the possibility of expanding what the *PC* can do) and having it work straight off without any tedious fiddling around and configuring.
Plug-ins	These are pieces of *software* that, when *installed*, enhance the *web* reading capacity of your *browser*. There are so many

different ways of 'broadcasting' information on the *WWW* or of making files *downloadable* that it would be impossible and inefficient for *browser software* to come equipped with ways of reading and displaying/playing everything. Instead we can choose to add specific plug-ins to the *browser* that will each perform a specific task. Most of these are available as *freeware* on the *web*, with more sophisticated versions that can be bought. The most commonly used types of plug-in are those that decompress *compressed* files and those that 'translate' and play back sound and video files over the *Internet*. Commonly, when you try to access a *web page* or *download* a file that requires a plug-in that you don't have, your *browser* will intervene and offer to take you to a page where you can *download* the appropriate plug-in. If you follow this *link* you are likely to be asked the type of computer and *browser* you are using and given instructions on how to *download* and *install* the plug-in.

POP　　　　Point of Presence or Post Office Protocol. A Point of Presence is the place where an *access provider* or *server* administrator has a computer which provides access to a *network* or the *Internet* and therefore dictates the telephone number your *modem* will need to dial to connect to a *network* or the *Internet*. So if an Internet company says they will soon have a POP in Birmingham, it means that they will soon have a telephone number in Birmingham and/or a place where leased lines can connect to their network. Post Office Protocol refers to the way *e-mail software* gets mail from a *mail server* (see *Protocol*).

Port　　　　An input/output socket through which the computer sends and receives information from a printer, keyboard, *mouse*, speaker, *monitor* etc. Serial or parallel ports differ only in the way information flows through them (in a single stream of one *bit* at a time through a serial port or in consecutive streams of 8 *bits* through a parallel port).

Portal　　　See *Subject-specific gateway*.

PowerPoint　See *Microsoft PowerPoint*.

PPP　　　　Point To Point Protocol. A *software application* that allows your computer to attach itself to a *server*.

Processor　　The processor chip is the part of the computer that does all the computing. Pentium and MMX are types of processor chips. In principle, the higher the figure attached to the processor the faster the computer can 'think' and react to commands. 286, 386 and 486 were the common processor speeds we spoke of for *PCs* before the faster Pentium chips. Now, commonly, a processor's capacity is measured in Megahertz.

Programme　Noun: a computer programme is a piece of *software* that has a specific task, such a clock or calculator, or which is a tool for the *user*, such as a *wordprocessor*. The words *application*, programme and *software* are more or less interchangeable. Verb: to programme a computer is to write a piece of *software* that asks the computer to perform a specific task. This may be very complex, such as *Windows* '95, or very simple, such as an on-screen clock.

Prompt

The *DOS* prompt is the flashing cursor next to a C:> on a black screen. (The letter indicates where the computer is 'thinking'; for example, if you have just performed a command in the windows directory, the prompt will show C:/WINDOWS:>) It is awaiting a typed command – this might be your *username* and password if you log onto a *network*, or it might be 'win' to open *Windows* from the *hard drive*. There is, of course, a whole vocabulary of commands that might be inputted, depending on what you want to ask of the computer. In practice, we can ignore *DOS* once we have bypassed it into a friendlier environment such as *Windows*.

Protocol

A set of rules that computers use when exchanging information with each other. The basic protocol for the *Internet* is *TCP/IP* (Transmission Control Protocol/Internet Protocol). Others include *HTTP* (Hypertext Transfer Protocol) for accessing *WWW* files on the *Internet*, SMTP (Simple Mail Transfer Protocol) for *e-mail*, NNTP (Network News Transfer Protocol) for newsgroups, *FTP* (File Transfer Protocol) for transferring files. All of these *Internet* protocols work on top of *TCP/IP*.

Pull-down menu

See *Drop-down menu*.

QuarkXpress

A page layout *software* product and integrated publishing package. See *Desktop Publishing*.

QuickTime

A *format* developed by Apple Macintosh used for adding video to *web sites*. The QuickTime Player is available as freeware and is necessary for viewing such files.

RAM

Random Access Memory. This is a type of memory that only exists when your computer is turned on and is used by the machine to hold open the programmes that are in use as well as the files upon which you are working. When you save a file you are saving it onto standard memory on the *hard drive* (measured in *bytes*) on a *floppy disk* or on your personal memory allocation on a *server*. Consequently, the size of the RAM of a machine significantly affects how many programmes you can run at a time (*multitasking*) and the size of any document(s) you are working on.

RealAudio

A method of playing sounds over the *Internet* without having to wait before you have *downloaded* the whole sound file first (sound files are naturally very large). RealAudio creates a *buffer* between the *server* supplying the sound file and your computer.

	The file begins to play without being completely *downloaded* almost as soon as *downloading* begins. The *plug-in RealPlayer* is available as *freeware* and a more sophisticated version can be paid for.
Real-time	Without any of the delays associated with long distance transmission. We speak of 'real-time' *virtual* experiences because they occur as they might do in reality, not slowed down nor speeded up, and responding to input instantaneously. A 'real-time voice interface', therefore, might normally be called a 'conversation'.
RealPlayer	Real.com *freeware*. See *RealAudio*.
Remote	'Remote' (as opposed to 'local') activities are those which occur digitally and physically away from the computer from which you participate in or control them.
Resolution	The number of *pixels* that a screen is able to display. Common Windows screen resolutions are 640 columns by 480 rows of *pixels*, 800×600, or 1024×768. The higher the resolution, the smaller the *pixels* on any given display.
RGB	Red, Green, Blue. Typical of pointless jargon – instead of referring to a colour *monitor*, some prefer to call your computer screen a RGB-*monitor*!
Robotics	A robot is 'a reprogrammable, multifunctional manipulator designed to move material, parts, tools, or specialised devices through various programmed motions for the performance of a variety of tasks' (Robot Institute of America, 1979). Robotics involves engineering various strategies, involving *hardware* and *software*, whereby *Artificial Intelligence* might interact with the human environment in a productive and useful manner.
ROM	Read Only Memory. A type of electronic memory that cannot be used to store *data*. Technically, all CDs are *CD-ROMs* because the *digital* information they contain, whether it be music or *software*, can only be 'read' by a CD player or CD drive, it cannot be altered and no other information can be 'recorded' to the CD, as it might to a *floppy disk*.
Scan	To *digitise* an image or other non-*digital* document using a *scanner*. See *Scanner*.
Scandisk	A *DOS programme* that checks your *hard* or *floppy disks* for faults and carries out necessary repairs. See *Bad sector*.
Scanner	A *hardware* device used to 'read' text or pictures into an associated computer *programme*, where the material can then be electronically manipulated. Hand-held and flat-bed scanners (i.e. desktop) are two types of scanner that are commonly available.
Screen capture	See *Capture*.
Script	A complete piece of *programming*, in whatever language, that

will perform a specific task. A *programme* or *application* is a complex construction of numerous scripts.

Scroll bar   The bar that appears on the right of most *wordprocessors'* screens (and similar *programmes*). It appears as a thin strip with an arrow at either extreme and a small 'button' somewhere in between. The position of this button indicates approximately where in the document you are at present and its size gives a rough idea of the size of the document (the smaller it is the larger the document). You can click on the arrows to 'scroll' forwards and backwards in the document or 'grab' the button (by clicking over it with the *mouse* key without unclicking) and sliding it up and down the scroll bar. Clicking elsewhere will cause the button to gravitate towards the *mouse* pointer effectively scrolling the document.

Scrolling (up or down) See *Scroll bar.*

SCUDD   The Standing Conference of University Drama Departments. A representative body that speaks for Lecturers in Drama, Theatre, Film, TV and Performing Arts in Higher Education Institutions in the UK.

Search Engines   Special *WWW* sites that offer a facility by which you can search the *web* or *Usenet* for information. Alta Vista (http://www.altavista.co.uk/), for example, provides a keyword search that scans every word of every page on the *web*. Yahoo! (http://www.yahoo.co.uk/) permits you to search by following ever-decreasing menus. Your *browser* will take you to a site featuring a number of *web* search engines. Click on 'Net search' if you use Netscape or 'Search' if you use Internet Explorer.

Server   The collection of *software* maintained and administered centrally and provided for the use of individuals who all log on to a *network*. The computers that are used to hold and provide the memory and *software* for the *network*.

SGML   Standard Generalized Markup Language. A *mark-up language* that makes it possible for different *software applications* to share and use the same information in their documents, even across computing *platforms*. Traditional document conversion programmes preserve any document's format, the idea behind SGML is to preserve the content and the structure (such as the layout of a document). This allows the information to be used and re-used by both publishing and non-publishing *applications*. See *Mark-up codes.*

Shareware   *Software* which you are given (with a computer magazine for example) or which you download free of charge to sample for a limited period of time, after which it is suggested you make a donation to the *software*'s author. Often such *software* will either cease to function, or will pop up nuisance reminders, after the trial period is over.

Shell
This is a *programme* that sets parameters within which any *application* to which it is attached can run.

Shockwave
A Macromedia *software* product that aids in the creation of animation for *web pages*. The Shockwave *plug-in* is necessary to view any page that has been created with this software.

Site
A *web site* (See *WWW*). This is a collection of *web pages*. Unlike a book you are invited to browse *web pages* in a non-linear fashion by following *links* between pages according to your whim. You access a site from its home page, which is usually the place you are taken by typing in the *web* address given in correspondence or advertisements. The *SCUDD* home page, for example, is at http://art.ntu.ac.uk/scudd/ From this page there are *links* to other pages on the same site and to the sites created and administered by the various members of *SCUDD* (from which other *links* could lead you much further – hence 'web').

SLIP
Serial Line Interface Protocol. An *application* that allows for a connection to another computer.

SMTP
Simple Mail Transfer Protocol. (See *TCP/IP* and *Protocol*)

Software
These are all the intangible elements of your computer held in memory on the *hard disk* (or by the *server* on a *network*) and, most commonly, are the *programmes* you use on the computer. The most essential software is the operating system (e.g. *DOS* or *Windows*) within which other software can run (your *wordprocessor* or *spreadsheets*). Software can be transferred to your computer via a *floppy disk* or a *CD-ROM*, or might be *downloaded* from the *Internet* as *Shareware* or *Freeware*.

Sound card
A piece of *hardware* that slots into your computer's *mother-board* enabling it to decipher and playback *digitised* sound (assuming the computer also has speakers).

Spam
A verb inspired by the Monty Python sketch, Spamming is the transmission of the same unwanted message, using *e-mail*, to whole collections of people on newsgroups.

Spreadsheet
A piece of *software* used predominantly for accounting and other numerically based tasks. The spreadsheet provides 'sheets' containing 'cells' each of which may contain text and/or numbers. Cells may also contain equations which calculate results from *data* placed in other cells or series of cells. A simple example might be a column of figures (inputted numbers) totalled in a single cell containing an equation relating to that column.

Stand-alone
Used to describe a computer that is not connected to a *network*, (on which *software* is provided by a *server*). Instead the stand-

alone has all its *software* on its *hard drive*. Many of us may have a stand-alone at home and work on a networked computer at work. A networked computer can still behave like a stand-alone as you do not need to log on to the network in order to use it, though it may have very little *software* on it other than the *operating system*.

Subject-Specific Gateway   A *web site* that provides access to a specific field of information.

Surf   We speak of 'surfing the net', i.e. browsing pages on the *Internet*.

SVGA (See *VGA*)   The S in SVGA stands for 'Super' and the *resolution* it can offer on screen can vary from 800×600 to 2048×1024 *pixels*, with colour count going from anything between 16 and 16 million colours per *pixel*. It is important to have a *monitor* that is compatible with the SVGA technology available in the computer to take full advantage of it.

System disk   A *floppy disk* containing a basic *operating system* from which a computer can *boot up*. See *BIOS* and *Booting up*.

Tables   Many *web pages* include embedded *HTML* code which dictates the layout of images and text on your screen. Using code for 'tables' allows the precise alignment of text or images alongside each other, and is a standard practice in most *web* design, with various levels of sophistication in its application.

TCP/IP   Transmission Control Protocol/Internet Protocol. Developed by the US military during the cold war, TCP/IP is the vehicle by which different computers are able to 'talk' to one another. Your *e-mail software* places its text and *attachment* into a TCP/IP 'vehicle' which then deposits these at the destination chosen.

Techno-phobia   The desire to ignore the overriding evidence that computing and *computer literacy* are becoming increasingly essential to our everyday existence. The inclination to come out in a cold sweat when faced with tasks such as switching on a computer. Remedies: publications such as this one.

Telnet   A form of *TCP/IP protocol*. The oldest way of using the *Internet*, by which you can tap into another computer elsewhere in the world and get it to execute your commands. It can be used to participate in chat groups or to access archives and documents stored in some foreign public access system.

Terminal   Your networked computer (where information 'terminates').

TIFF   Tagged Image File Format. A *bitmap* graphic file *format* and one of the most widely used bitmap graphic format in the printing world. See *BMP*.

Tool bar   This is usually a collection of *icons* across the top border of the on-screen 'window' of any *programme*, usually underneath a *menu bar*. By 'depressing' these small 'buttons' with a click of the *mouse* you can activate that particular tool. You can get rid of the whole bar, or customise it, in many cases.

Tower	The casing of the computer which is constructed to stand upright rather than flat. This is purely a design feature and makes no difference to the type or power of computer you have. It saves space on a desk (or can more easily be placed underneath the desk).
Traffic	See *Bandwidth* and *TCP/IP*.
Transparent	Anything in *software* behaviour that occurs without your being aware (i.e. most of it).
True-type fonts	Many computer *fonts* are designed for greater readability on the screen in front of you. True-type fonts are not *pixel*-based and can be reproduced on *hard-copy* as they appear on screen.
TWAIN	Technology Without An Interesting Name. No, really.
UNIX	An *operating system* largely used for science and engineering *applications* and computer *networks*. It was developed to allow one *server* to service many different *users* at the same time.
Upload	To send files from your own computer onto someone else's or, most frequently, onto the *Internet* if you maintain a *web site* on the *WWW*. See *Download*.
UPS	Uninterruptible Power Supply.
URL	Uniform Resource Locator. This is the 'address' of a *web page*, or that of the 'home page' (front door/foyer) of a *web site*. A URL will usually be of the order http://www.domain.ac.uk/ first/page1.html which translates as 'Using *Hypertext* transfer *protocol* on the *Word Wide Web* the UK based academic *domain* provides in its "first" subdirectory a page called "page1" written in *HTML*'. Whilst most of the world uses, for example, ac.uk and co.fr to indicate an academic or commercial site in a specific country, US based sites may just end in, for example, 'edu', 'com' or 'org' (academic, commercial or business) and this fashion has now caught on elsewhere, especially the 'dot.com' (see *.com*). Because it can be taken for granted that a *web page* will use *http* most URLs are given as simply, for example, 'www.channel4.com'.
User	Someone using a computer. You.
User-friendly	With no irony intended, this is the term applied to *GUI* type *programmes* that allow you to click on buttons and *drop-down menus* and fill in *dialogue boxes* to get the computer to do what you want it to do. The 'unfriendly' versions were those that required you to type in commands at a *prompt* or which were all text based with no images.
Username	A code which represents you (the *user*) which is required when logging on to a *network*. A password is usually also demanded to ensure that only you use your *network* account and have access to your documents.
User support	Strategies for offering assistance to *users* when their *IT*

confrontations become all too much. These may include manuals, help files, in-built tutorials, *web pages*, *web* tutorials or phone lines to real people.

Usenet
The massive collection of newsgroups available on the *Internet*, though you'll often be hard pressed to find any news on these chat lines. Using your *browser* you can select a group and 'subscribe' to it by selecting the appropriate command in the appropriate menu and *download* all new messages on it. You can then post a message to it or continue to log into it to read the international chat on your topic of choice.

VAX Notes
A rather outmoded computer-mediated conferencing system which permits different *users* to deposit and respond to notes on a number of indexed subject areas. Mailing lists and the *Usenet* provide a similar facility *online*.

VBA
Visual Basic for Applications. This facility provides the power to programme *Microsoft Access*, of which it is a component part. Users may create VBA programmes to control the input of *data* into *database* tables in *MS Access*. See *Microsoft Access*.

VGA
Followed the *EGA* (adopting the name Very enhanced Graphics Adapter). Gave the *monitor* a display of 640×480 *pixels* and therefore greater clarity.

Virtual
Any event, meeting or activity that is performed using computers by anybody or by any group of people, which occurs in what might be deemed as *cyberspace* (that is to say within the *digital processing* activity of a computer or of interconnected communicating computers) might be deemed a 'virtual' event, meeting or activity.

Virus
Very Important Resource Under Siege (in this case the acronym was used before anyone decided what it might stand for). A computer virus is a form of *software* that has been created with the malicious aim of causing damage to other people's computers. Like all *programmes*, once activated it will continue to carry out its instructions until it is switched off. Often, however, viruses are constructed with no off-switch. The damage usually involves destroying *data* and software. Some viruses activate once they have entered a particular type of system, others lie in wait on your hard drive until a specific *user* event (calling up a certain *programme*, for example) or a particular date (the Michaelangelo strain, for example, which waits until the artist's birthday). These *programmes* are called viruses because they can spread and infect computers by being passed on inadvertently on *floppy disks* or via the *Internet*. There are as many hoaxes as there are true viruses. A virus cannot exist within a simple text file such as an *e-mail*, but might come as an *attachment* to an *e-mail* (an '*executable* file',

for example, which comes to you unsolicited, may be suspect). Slower moving viruses are called *worms*.

VRML Virtual Reality Modelling Language. An *application* that gives a 3-D effect to pictures sometimes allowing you to apparently move through them as you interact with the *programme*.

WAN Wide Area Network, as opposed to *LAN*. The *Internet* is the most obvious example.

WAP Wireless Application Protocol. This is the standard *protocol* for applications that use wireless technology such as mobile phones and other hand-held devices.

WAV WAVeform sound format. Microsoft's *format* for encoding sound files, which therefore carry the wav *extension*.

Web, Web site, Web page. See *WWW*.

Webcasting Broadcasting (usually live events such as performances or concerts) across the *WWW* for viewing on computer screens.

Webserver See *Server*.

WWW The World Wide Web. This is a collection of millions of '*web pages*' written in a (relatively) simple *programming* language called *HTML*. The *web* is a subsection of the *Internet*, though these terms are frequently considered interchangeable. You access the *web* on a computer with a *modem* or connected to a *network* with an *Internet* facility. The *software* necessary to view *web pages* is called a *browser*. (The two main ones are Netscape Navigator and Microsoft Internet Explorer – both available as *freeware* to individual *users*.) A *web page* may have *links* to other pages and these appear most commonly as underlined and coloured text which you click on using the *mouse* pointer to be taken by the *browser* to the *link*ed page. Pictures may also be *links*. When the cursor hovers over a *link* it turns from a pointer to a hand with an extended index finger – indicating that should you click there using the *mouse* you will be taken elsewhere. *Links* may be to other pages on the same *site*, or to pages on some other *site*.

Windows A Microsoft *software* product used uniquely in PCs (though compatible Macs can run it). Windows is an extension of *DOS*, the PC's *operating system*, and it sits as an interface between us and the computer's power. From the 'desktop' we can open up individual 'windows', such as our own documents or specific *programmes*. Windows allows us to control the environment usually by pointing a *mouse* at an *icon*, using the *mouse* to bring down a *menu* and selecting an item or by opening *dialogue boxes*, into which we can type or click the desired function/ alterations. The Amiga and the Mac have similar environments, providing 'windows', though these systems are not Windows (with a capital W!). Windows 3.1 was the standard for many years before Microsoft brought out the much improved Windows '95 environment which functioned in much the same manner with slight improvements, better *multitasking*, a fax sending and receiving facility, greater emphasis on connecting to the *Internet*, and some changes in vocabulary. Windows '98 and Windows 2000 were improvements on this basic development.

Wordprocessor A piece of *software* that facilitates the manipulation of text (and the inclusion of images and *spreadsheet* elements into a text document). The *digital* typewriter, if you will.

Worm A type of *virus* which creates damage at a gradual pace. See *Virus*.

WYSIWYG 'What you see is what you get.' WYSIWYG *programmes*, such as some *wordprocessor* and *spreadsheets*, boast simply that the layout, style and font chosen on screen will be exactly what appears on your *hard copy* when you print out your document. This is more or less standard today.

XML EXtensible Markup Language. XML is a 'dialect' of the *SGML mark-up language*. It enables generic *SGML* to be served, received, and processed on the *web*. See *Mark-up codes* and *SGML*.

ZIP Zone Information Protocol. An *application* that allows for the compression of *executable* files for ease and speed of transfer over the *Internet*. To *download* these you first need to *download* and *install* an unzipping *plug-in* for your *browser*.

4.2: Bibliography and further reading

Aronowitz, S and Menser, M., 1996. 'On Cultural Studies, Science, and Technology', in S. Aronowitz (ed.), *Technoscience and Cyberculture*. New York: Routledge.

Artaud, A., 1970. *The Theatre and its Double*. London: Calder and Boyars.

Barrett, E. (ed.), 1988. *Text, ConText, and HyperText: Writing for the Computer*. Cambridge, Massachusetts: MIT Press.

Barrett, E., 1992. *Sociomedia: Multimedia, Hypermedia and the Social Construction of Knowledge*. Cambridge, Massachusetts: MIT Press.

Batty, M., 1999. *A Very Basic Introduction to IT*. University of Exeter Drama Department. (Unpublished)

Boden, M., 1981. *Artificial Intelligence and Natural Man*. New York: Basic Books.

Carson, C.J and Bratton, J., 2000. *Cambridge King Lear CD-ROM: Text and Performance Archive*. Cambridge: Cambridge University Press.

Dixon, S., 1995. *Chameleons: Theatrical Experiments in Style, Genre and Multimedia* [CD-ROM]. Published/ Distributed by *Studies in Theatre Production*. Exeter University Press.

Dixon, S., 1999. *Chameleons 2: Theatre in A Movie Screen* [CD-ROM]. Published/Distributed by *TDR: The Drama Review*, 43 (1), NYU/MIT Press.

Essif, L., 1994. 'Introducing the "Hyper" Theatrical Subject: The *Mise en Abyme* of Empty Space'. *Journal of Dramatic Theory and Criticism*, 9(1), University of Kansas.

Harnad, S., 1999. 'The Future of Scholarly Skywriting', in A. Scammell (ed.), *i in the Sky: Visions of the information future*.

Heckell, P., 1982. *The Elements of Friendly Software Design*. New York: Warner.

Hutcheon, L., 1988. *A Poetics of Postmodernism: History, Theory, Fiction*. New York: Routledge.

Kolb, D., 1996. 'Discourse Across Links', in C. Ess (ed.), *Philosophical Perspectives on Computer-Mediated Communication*. Albany: State University of New York Press.

Landow, G.P., 1992. *Hypertext: The Convergence of Contemporary Critical Theory and Technology*. Baltimore, Maryland: John Hopkins University Press.

Landow, G.P. (ed.), 1994. *Hyper/Text/Theory*. Baltimore, Maryland: John Hopkins University Press.

Laurel, B. (ed.), 1990. *The Art of Human-Computer Interface Design*. Reading, Massachusetts: Addison-Wesley.

Laurel, B., 1991. *Computers as Theater*. Reading, Massachusetts: Addison-Wesley.

Lycouris, S., 1996. *Destabilising dancing: tensions between the theory and practice of improvisational performance*. (Unpublished PhD thesis) Guildford: University of Surrey.

Murray, J.H., 1997. *Hamlet on the Holodeck: The Future of Narrative in Cyberspace*. Free Press.

Norman, D.A., 1991. 'Foreword', in: B. Laurel, 1991.

Norman, D.A. and Draper, S. (eds), 1986. *User Centred Systems Design: New Perspectives on Human-Computer Interaction*. Hillsdale, NJ: Lawrence Erlbaum.

Quittner, J. and Slatalla, M., 1995. *Masters of Deception*. London: Vintage.

Rutsky, R.L., 1999. *High Techne: Art and Technology from the Machine Aesthetic to the Posthuman*. Minneapolis and London: University of Minnesota Press.

Ryle, G., 1979. *On Thinking*. Oxford: Blackwell.

Shu, N.C., 1992. *Visual Programming*. New York: Van Nostrand Reinhold.

Smith, B., 1997. 'Live Art's Digital Horizons'. *Literary & Linguistic Computing* 12 (4).

Smith, B., 1998. 'Overload and underload in our digital future'. *The Digital Demotic,* OHC (10), King's College London.

Smith, J., 1999a. 'Prolegomena to any future e-publishing model'. ICCC/IFIP Electronic Publishing Conference 1999, *Redefining the Information Chain, New Ways and Voices*. ICCC Publishing. URL: http://library.ukc.ac.uk/library/papers/jwts/Prolegomena.htm

Smith, J., 1999b. 'The Deconstructed Journal – a new model for Academic Publishing'. *Learned Publishing*. 12 (2). Association of Learned and Professional Society Publishers.

URL: http://library.ukc.ac.uk/library/papers/jwts/d-journal.htm

Vaughan, T., 1994. *Multimedia: Making it Work*. Berkeley, California: Osborne McGraw-Hill.

Warkentin, E., 1997. 'Consumer Issues and the Scholarly Journal'. *Canadian Journal of Communication* 22 (3/4).

Web Resources

GENERAL

Arts and Humanities Data Service – http://ahds.ac.uk
AHDS: Creating A Viable Scholarly Data Resource – http://ahds.ac.uk/viable.htm
AHDS Publication Series: Guides to Good Practice in the Creation and Use of Digital Resources –
    http://ahds.ac.uk/guides.htm
Performing Arts Data Service – http://www.pads.ahds.ac.uk
Visual Arts Data Service – http://www.vads.ahds.ac.uk

TECHNICAL ADVICE AND RESOURCES

Apache HTTP Server Project – http://www.apache.org/httpd.html
Jakob Nielson's Website of Usable Information Technology – http://www.useit.com
Microsoft Active Server Pages FAQ –http://msdn.microsoft.com/library/backgrnd/html/
    msdn_aspfaq.htm
Microsoft Online Library – http://msdn.microsoft.com/library/default.asp
MySQL Pages – http://www.mysql.com
PHP Pages – http://www.php.net
Setting up Database Driven Websites – http://www.devshed.com/Server_Side/Administration/
    Database/

EXISTING WEB RESOURCES

crasis: the trans/form and string projects – http://www.ad406.dial.pipex.com/
Le Theatre de la foires a Paris – http://foires.net
Liss Fain Dance web site – http://www.lissfaindance.org/
The Live Art Archive – http://art.ntu.ac.uk/liveart/
Sound Journal – http://www.ukc.ac.uk/sdfva/sound-journal/
The WWW Virtual Library – http://www.vlib.org
The WWW Virtual Library: Theatre and Drama – http://vl-theatre.com